THE AGE OF UNPEACE

The Age of Unpeace

How Connectivity Causes Conflict

MARK LEONARD

BANTAM PRESS

TRANSWORLD PUBLISHERS
Penguin Random House, One Embassy Gardens,
8 Viaduct Gardens, London SW11 7BW
www.penguin.co.uk

Transworld is part of the Penguin Random House group of companies
whose addresses can be found at global.penguinrandomhouse.com

Penguin
Random House
UK

First published in Great Britain in 2021 by Bantam Press
an imprint of Transworld Publishers

A CIP catalogue record for this book
is available from the British Library.

ISBN 9781787634657 (hb)
9781787634664 (tpb)

Typeset in 11.33/16.46pt Minion Pro by Jouve (UK), Milton Keynes
Printed and bound in Great Britain by Clays Ltd, Elcograf S.p.A.

The authorized representative in the EEA is Penguin Random House Ireland,
Morrison Chambers, 32 Nassau Street, Dublin D02 YH68.

Penguin Random House is committed to a sustainable
future for our business, our readers and our planet. This book
is made from Forest Stewardship Council® certified paper.

For Mum and Dad
For Berni and Annele
For John, Marjorie, Richard and Andrew
For Graham, Susie and Guy
For Miriam, Phiroze and Isaac
For Jakob and Noa
For Gabrielle

CONTENTS

THE CONNECTIVITY CONUNDRUM

We may be on the cusp of a new, silent pandemic. Like Covid-19, it is rampaging across the planet, spreading exponentially, exploiting the cracks in our networked world and constantly mutating to evade our defences. But unlike the virus which pits all of humanity against a disease, this new pandemic is being deliberately transmitted from human to human. It is not a biological force, but a set of toxic behaviours that are multiplying like a virus. The connections between people and countries are becoming weapons.

Just look at our response to Covid. There have not been enough vaccines, masks and gowns to go round and, rather than working together to increase global supplies, countries have used their stocks to bully others. When the virus first struck, the Chinese government hoarded medicines, masks and PPE. And when it spread, these supplies were used to bribe and to blackmail. China's allies – Brazil, Serbia, and Italy – were showered with masks and vaccines. But more critical states – like Australia, France, the Netherlands, Sweden and the USA – faced threats to withhold supplies unless their governments changed policy.[1]

These toxic connections are not just about trade. In America when the Black Lives Matter protests raged over the George Floyd murder, a wave of African social media posts called for violence against the 'fascist police'. It looked like a global political awakening, but it was orchestrated by troll factories in Ghana and Nigeria funded by the Russian state.

Conflict over technology itself is affecting the world's biggest companies. Google and Huawei had worked together closely for years, building a partnership between the most successful handset maker and the most widely used operating system. But when America put the Chinese handset maker on a banned list, Google banned Huawei from its Android platform, leaving millions unable to update their phones and plunging China's tech giant into crisis.

Even states that are allies often seem to end up at loggerheads. For example, in December 2020 British supermarkets ran out of fruit and vegetables when the French government closed its borders. The ban on British lorries was ostensibly to control Covid, but it also put the squeeze on Downing Street in the Brexit endgame.

And while superpowers flex their muscles, weaker countries are making use of similar tactics to strike back. In the same year, the Iranian Navy seized oil tankers to protest against crippling sanctions, their piracy designed to break support for a financial blockade. A few months earlier, in nearby Turkey the president opened his country's border to Greece, urging millions of Syrian refugees to seek a better life in Europe. His goal was not to help them follow their dreams but to use the threat of a wave of refugees to extort concessions from the European Union.

What do Chinese bullying, Russian trolling, American regulation, French blockades, Iranian piracy, and Turkish blackmail have in common? They were not random accidents – like an asteroid falling from the sky or an earthquake – but new types of political violence. Each was a weapon perfectly evolved to exploit a weakness in our connected world. Each time one country uses one, another reciprocates, creating a deadly spiral of tensions. And as we get further into the twenty-first century their use is spreading to pandemic proportions.

UNWAR AND UNPEACE

This is a short book with a simple idea: that the connections that knit the world together are also driving it apart. In a world where war between nuclear powers is too dangerous even to contemplate, countries are waging conflicts by manipulating the very things that link them together.[2] Great power politics has become like a loveless marriage where the couple can't stand each other's company but are unable to get divorced. And as with an unhappy couple, it is the things that we shared during the good times that become the means to harm during the bad ones. In a collapsing marriage, vindictive partners will use the children, the dog and the holiday home to hurt each other. In geopolitics, it is trade, finance, the movement of people, pandemics, climate change and above all the internet that are being weaponized.[3] And, as will become apparent later, it is connectivity itself that gives people the opportunity to fight, the reasons to compete, and the arsenal to deploy.

Rather than eliminating competition between countries, the deep interdependence seems to fuel it. Economic coercion is nothing new, but the hidden wiring of globalization is. And the ways that it is being manipulated give sanctions, blockades and PR campaigns a viral quality and deadliness that did not exist before our world was defined by networks. Although the journalist Thomas Friedman claimed that our globalized world is flat, it is in fact just the opposite – an uneven and mountainous network. Some countries are more central to the system than others. They can cut rival nations off and use their control of hubs to assert their power – as America does with the dollar and its control of the internet or China with its manufacture of medical supplies and access to rare earths. But even weak countries can target the strong with the right leverage as Iran is doing by blocking shipping routes or Turkey by using refugees as pawns.

Should we think of these new conflicts as 'connectivity wars'? Sort of, but not quite.[4] The alternation between war and peace has shaped human history, defining the borders of our countries, and influencing the nature of our social contracts, the structure of our economies and the purpose of our politics. It has captured our imaginations and inspired some of our greatest poems and novels. However, Tolstoy would not be able to write a masterpiece like *War and Peace* if he were alive today. Nobody could, because the distinction between war and peace has broken down.

The rules of war state that it should take place between sovereign states. It should begin with a declaration and end with a peace treaty. And the combatants should be soldiers who are clearly distinguished by their uniforms.

Those kinds of conventional wars have all but disappeared. They haven't happened in Europe or America since the Second World War. And although the wars in the Middle East and Africa are tragic, the number of people they kill is tiny in historical terms. For the last couple of decades more people have committed suicide than died in armed combat.[5]

Carl von Clausewitz famously called war the continuation of politics by other means. But in a nuclear age the price of war is unfathomable. That is why connectivity conflicts are becoming the 'other means' of global politics. They are less costly. They are more effective. As a result they are becoming more prevalent. And as they proliferate across the world they are killing many more people than conventional warfare.

Rather than playing out on the land, air and seas, the new struggles exist on the internet, border controls, technology, supply chains and our financial system. They have brought conflict back from the periphery of the global economy to its very core; Europe and America are just as affected as Africa or Latin America. The combatants in these struggles have changed too: in the old days only a few great powers could fight across continents but nowadays millions of people can inflict harm on one another through the internet or terrorism. The victims are civilians rather than soldiers, and they number in the millions rather than the thousands.

Because connectivity conflicts do not produce the kind of dramatic shareable video footage beloved by social media, most people think they're less lethal than conventional military conflicts. But just because we can't see body bags does not mean that these conflicts are not deadly. In fact, they've already blighted the lives of hundreds of millions of people.

Sanctions, population expulsions and trade wars have been around for centuries but until the world became organized around global supply chains, internet politics and a dollarized financial system, it was hard to strangle foreign economies and societies at so little cost to oneself. Sanctions have already killed hundreds of thousands – from Venezuela and Iran to Sudan and North Korea – primarily by restricting access to food, medicines and electricity. Millions of civilians have been forced deliberately from their homes for political reasons in the last few decades, from Cuba and Kosovo to Libya and Turkey, to name just a few. Trade wars have cost tens of millions of jobs – from Russia and China to Germany and Canada – while cyber attacks have the potential to disrupt entire countries. The US Department of Homeland Security has identified sixty-five facilities in the US against which a single cyber attack would cause 'catastrophic harm' – defined as 'causing or having the likelihood to cause $50 billion in economic damage, 2,500 fatalities,

or a severe degradation of our national security'. Some of the most insidi-
ous cyber attacks to date have been attempts to hack democratic elections
(between the autumn of 2016 and the spring of 2019, there were attempts
to interfere with national elections in twenty democracies representing
1.2 billion people).[6]

If we add all of these up, it's clear that the body count for connectivity
wars dwarfs that of conventional wars in the twenty-first century. Over
the last two decades fewer than 70,000 people a year on average have
been killed in military conflicts[7] – while millions have been harmed by
connectivity wars. And it's only going to get worse.

But although connectivity conflicts are more common, more effective and more deadly than conventional wars, we don't really recognize
that they are happening – and don't even have a term to describe them.
As a result the conventional wisdom is that we live in a golden age of
peace.

It is true that these new kinds of attack do not match the conventional definition of war. But how can we close our eyes to the tension
and violence that is ripping through our world every day? Once we start
to count the millions of casualties every year we can hardly describe our
era as one of peace.

In fact, there is a word which starts to capture our liminal condition –
suspended somehow between a state of war and one of peace. Academics
such as Lucas Kello who work on cyber were looking for a term that
describes the grey zone that their world was stuck in, where every day
they saw millions of attacks which fell short of conventional war. They
rehabilitated a beautiful Anglo-Saxon word to describe disorder on the
internet: unpeace.[8] And as violence spreads from the internet to trade,
finance, migration and beyond, their word provides a perfect encapsu-
lation of our condition. We are having to get used to an unstable,
crisis-prone world of perpetual competition and endless attacks between
competing powers. Welcome to the age of unpeace.

THERE AND BACK AGAIN

I am maybe one of the people least well equipped to spot the fact that we live in an age of unpeace. Every aspect of my family's history and identity has been shaped by the imprint of war while my own life has been entirely defined by its absence.

My father's father was born into a modest background in late Victorian Britain. He lied about his age to fight in the First World War and his life was saved by being gassed and taken to hospital. My father was evacuated as an eight-year-old in the Second World War and was so traumatized by the experience that he became a conscientious objector rather than doing military service in the 1950s. His experiences motivated an interest in politics and as an adult he was one of a group of sixty-nine Labour MPs who defied the party whip to vote for Britain's membership of the European Community.

My mother was born in 1944 in a convent in France where her German Jewish parents were hiding. She lived in France for a few years (where her father remained) before returning to Germany in 1950. Her surviving relatives are peppered across the world. And when you bring any of them together you need to be ready for a conversation that includes at least English, French and German.

Like many in Europe I am part of the first generation in my family for 150 years not to face war, exile or even extermination. My life has been full of opportunities unimaginable for earlier generations. Having grown up in Brussels in the 1980s with a British father and a French-born German-Jewish mother, it was my European identity that brought unity and meaning to my family's fragmented history. One of the most influential people in my early life was my maternal grandmother, Gertrud Heidelberger, a Holocaust survivor who was orphaned at the age of ten. She taught herself seven European languages and even in old age could recite the poems of Dante, Heine, Keats, and Wordsworth. I grew up learning how the different and often violent histories reflected by those national poets could be united by a common European story about the future. I believed that a sense of shared European culture and destiny was not only possible but necessary to avoid the catastrophes of the past. My work has reflected those family lessons.

In 2005 I wrote a book called *Why Europe Will Run the 21st Century*, a love letter to a project that had buried war, brought waves of countries out of dictatorship and into democracy and expanded the horizons of hundreds of millions of people.[9] I have also tried to understand other world cultures to make the foreign more familiar. I spent several years studying the intellectual emancipation of China, writing a book called *What Does China Think?* which explored the big debates on capitalism, politics and globalization in this rising superpower.[10] And in 2007, I set up a European think-tank with a mission to promote conflict resolution through diplomacy rather than on the battlefield.[11] I recruited staff from over twenty countries and established offices in seven countries, with our biggest in London. My family life, my career, and my worldview were all buoyed up by the rising tide of internationalism.

But in 2016, with Britain voting to leave the European Union and Donald Trump winning the White House, the tide went out. I felt shipwrecked, and many people, companies and families were left stranded. For me, the world's journey from nationalism to globalism – and back again – has not been an abstract matter. Why did so many people reject the forces that had made my life so much safer and more fulfilled than those of my ancestors? How could they want to go back to an earlier age that did not benefit from these human links and technological advances? If we stick with a conventional twentieth-century analysis, it's hard to understand *why* we live in a world in which scientific knowledge, connectivity, and an awareness of a shared destiny are not enough to bring people together to solve urgent common problems. So how do we explain the last five years?

That is the question that I have asked myself every day since 2016. In my search for answers, I've drawn on political science, history, sociology, economics and psychology and talked to network scientists, artists, anthropologists, and even priests, among many others. My research has taken me from Facebook's headquarters in Silicon Valley to facial recognition labs in China; from meetings with the Turkish president in his sumptuous new palace to military installations in Hawaii. I've talked to billionaires in Davos and unemployed labourers in Brexit Britain. I've met Iranian Revolutionary Guards and Saudi princes; and exchanged ideas with some of the most active builders of the connected world, such as George Soros and Peter Thiel. I went into this process expecting to write a defence of the open world but the deeper I dug the more complex my thinking became. I started having some nagging questions. What if the process that brings us together is actually what *causes* segregation and conflict? What if the growing divisions in the globalized world are not a bug in the system but one of its intrinsic features?

OPPORTUNITY, REASONS AND WEAPONS

Globalization – that is, the connectivity of people, markets, technology and ideas – offered so much to the world. This book is about what happened when it broke its promise, and what this betrayal means for us all. The problem is simple to articulate but one that I find very difficult to accept. We can't have 'one world' because becoming more interlinked is not simply a source of understanding and togetherness. It is also the cause of ever more bitter division and conflict.[12] People have claimed for some time that connectivity can be used for good or ill. They have maintained that interdependence does not always stop war. And some have even written about how it has been weaponized. But I have discovered something even more concerning: that it is connectivity itself that drives us apart. It gives people the *opportunity* for conflict; *reasons* to fight each other; and a lot of *weapons* with which to inflict harm.

Let's start with the *opportunity*. At the turn of the millennium, like many people I had hoped the internet and globalization would provide the impetus for a global political consciousness. Connectivity would spread global understanding. Trade would bind us all together through global supply chains, making war increasingly costly, even irrational. Science would replace emotion as the basis for decisions about the future of humanity. And law would replace war as a means of settling disputes over everything from trade and the environment to data and human rights. Governments set about ripping down walls, dissolving borders, signing trade deals, building roads, railways, pipelines, airports; and wove a world wide web that bound the entire planet. Globalization has literally strung us together: 64 million kilometres of highways; 2 million kilometres of pipelines; 1.2 million kilometres of railways; and 750,000 kilometres of undersea internet cables. By contrast, there are just 250,000 kilometres of international borders dividing us.[13] Twenty years ago there were only 16 million people online but now it is half of humanity (and by 2022 the connected population could reach 6 billion).[14] Every day almost 1.5 billion people log on to Facebook and 500 million tweets are posted on Twitter.[15]

In a connected world, people don't have an option to keep themselves to themselves: everyone is in each other's face. This allows nations and people to work together, to trade, to learn from each other and develop bonds of friendship. But connectivity also creates opportunities for greater competition between nations and people. As the great sociologist Anthony Giddens has pointed out, social media has made a reality of the global village, where people form personal friendships and intimate relationships, but where we also contend with bullies, gossip, innuendo, deception and violence.[16]

As the world becomes ever more crowded and digitally connected, these points of contact create more potential sources of conflict, and supply more opportunities to interfere in each other's affairs. Connected networks are the transmission belts – allowing people and nations to turn our open societies against themselves. And they also allow countries to compare themselves to each other, to copy each other and in the process spiral into competition. As with so many things, the ancient Greeks understood the tension best. They had a single word for a medicine that could end up poisoning its patient, *pharmakon*. The tragedy of our generation is that the forces that have united humankind are also dividing us and threatening to destroy us. But just because connectivity creates an opportunity for conflict, it does not mean that conflict needs to happen. The root causes of tensions between countries are fear, greed, and the desire for power or status. And connectivity can enhance them all.

My second theme in the book is why connectivity gives us the *reasons* to fight. We have known for a long time that it has a dark side as well as a light one – allowing competition as well as cooperation. I have come to the conclusion that connectivity tips the scales in favour of competition by changing the way that people and countries think of their identity and interests. In this book I explore how digital connectivity is bringing out the competitive side of human nature – leading to much more polarized societies, fuelling an epidemic of envy and also taking away control.

Digital media have fragmented reality so dramatically that there is no agreement on the truth, which means that societies are not just divided by different opinions but also by different facts. It has taken me too long to understand that so many people interpreted the last few decades in a completely different way from me. In my life, the liberalization of travel and trade and the EU's rules on free movement have only brought opportunity. I have enjoyed so many experiences in different countries, tasted new foods, been able to recruit better and more interesting staff, and could think about a career where the best jobs in the world were open to me. But to many other people in the same period, international links opened the door to the off-shoring of their jobs. They invited into the country well-qualified migrants who would work for less money, crowd their hospitals and schools, drive up house prices and introduce different languages and shops to our high streets. They provided new routes for financial crises, terrorism and pandemics to enter our communities and new standards by which to judge our response. And our culture changed so profoundly that some profess to fear becoming 'strangers in their own lands'. In other words, many of the things I saw as bringing peace and opportunity have made others feel vulnerable and poorer. Because we consumed different media and interpreted their messages in different ways we did not draw on a shared conception of reality. Happily ensconced within my own bubble, I was not confronted with the growing inequality, envy and sense of loss of control that connectivity was fuelling in parallel bubbles.

Social media have also fuelled envy on an industrial scale by opening everyone's lives up for comparison. Friedrich Nietzsche first argued that expanding travel, trade and communications in the nineteenth century created an 'age of comparison'. He could see that a new global consciousness would lead people to compare their own country's ideas, customs and culture with others' – and to reject their lot when it was lacking. But for Nietzsche the notion was abstract, a battle of ideas rather than a daily grind that relentlessly exposed the limitations of our own lives in comparison with the most privileged and successful in the world. Economists have shown how globalization fuels tensions by turbo-charging inequality and creating losers with a stake in overthrowing the system. Foreign policy experts have told us how connectivity can lead to geopolitical tensions by changing the balance of power. Just as Germany's trade-powered rise led to tensions with the British empire, so too is China's rise creating frictions with the USA. But it is comparisons at the level of individuals which have been most dramatically altered. When I was a child we would compare our experience to our neighbours' or our parents' lives – but nowadays every aspect of our existence can be benchmarked against (sometimes fictionalized) depictions of the most privileged and successful people in the whole world. How can our lives ever match up to those standards? The result is permanent resentment.

Connectivity increasingly makes people feel the world is beyond their control. As you can imagine, in the wake of Brexit I often get mocked for my book on Europe. Many people see the title *Why Europe Will Run the 21st Century* as an act of hubris. And looking back on it, the title of the book was indeed absurd. I don't regret the praise I lavished on the European ideal, but it was wrong to imply that any sole power could run a world defined by globalization. After all, the core feature of our interconnected planet is the loss of control. This is keenly felt by nations who struggle to tie down mobile capital, to regulate digital titans, to limit climate change or avoid exploitation by continental superpowers. But it is also felt by individuals in the face of unaccountable algorithms, economic and demographic change or political elites they no longer feel represent them.

I try to show how the convergence of these forces is leading to greater conflict *within* nations, driving a new politics of identity and envy that was reflected in the Brexit referendum and Trump's America. I also show how these trends are leading to more conflict *between* nations. A new tribalism and sense of victimhood has come together with a new topography of power in an age of global networks. I explore how countries as diverse as Iran and Saudi Arabia, Russia and Turkey have reinvented their foreign policies to compete in the new age.

My third big theme is to explore how the ties that bind us have been turned into *weapons*. The examples at the beginning of this chapter reveal some of the hidden wiring of our globalized world, and how it is being used to drive people apart. We can see that whoever is in power today – a Biden or a Trump, a Chinese dictator or a French democrat – will increasingly manipulate the ties of globalization to seek power for themselves and harm others.

The forces of connectivity intended to bring the world together have metamorphosed into the battlegrounds of a global tug of war. There is an economic realm defined by trade supply chains, currencies and financial systems, as well as natural resources and energy. There is a contest over global infrastructure linked to the flow of energy and data. There is a technological world where participants will fight over intellectual property and information. There will be battles over migration and refugees and the transit agreements that regulate their flow. And global institutions will continue to be a battleground rather than a check on competition. Trade wars, sanctions, cyber attacks, fake news and the expulsion of refugees have shown how leaders can manipulate these links between nations to inflict pain on others and get ahead themselves. All these points of contact between peoples form the battlegrounds for a permanent conflict that pits nation against nation.

In this new global contest countries are drawing on whatever leverage they have to hand. Russia is using gas supplies to blackmail its neighbours, and interfering in elections; Turkey is threatening to open its borders and expel refugees; Saudi Arabia is supporting paramilitary organizations and funding Wahhabi mosques in other countries; India is complaining about 'data colonialism' and excluding Chinese internet companies from its market. But the three biggest players are the United States, China and Europe. The USA relies on the reach of the dollar to police access to the global financial system and its control of the internet to put the planet under surveillance.

China is building roads, railways and cables, and using its enormous cash reserves and the profits from a protected home market, to link itself to all other countries around the world on terms favourable to itself. The European Union uses the size of its market and its bureau-cratic capacity to develop a rule-book for global connectivity. As we enter a period of total connectivity, the three biggest powers have differ-ent views of what is at stake. Each has different weapons, philosophies and ways of looking at the world. The shape of our global order will be defined by the battle between these three empires of connectivity.

GREAT RESET

Many of my friends think we are facing the fight of our lives, a struggle to save the open world order. Politics for them no longer split 'left' from 'right', but 'open' from 'closed'.[17] The big questions are now: welcome migrants or build walls? Free trade or protectionism? Modern values or a return to tradition? Petty conflicts between party elites have been transcended by a new schism that seems to explain all divisions from the bedroom to the boardroom.

The idea of a divide between 'open' and 'closed' gives politics a gran-deur and simplicity that has been absent since the end of the Cold War. Populism, economic insecurity and social media have laid the founda-tions for a political counter-revolution that has overturned the consensus of the last generation. The solution for some is to fight back and recover lost gains. Defeat Trump and Johnson. End austerity. Regulate Big Tech. As I write this, I have a copy of *The Economist* beside me. The cover proclaims, 'Goodbye Globalism', and asks, 'Has Covid-19 killed globali-sation?' It claims 'the greatest era of world history' has been pummelled by three body blows: the financial crash of 2008; the Sino-American trade war; and Covid-19. But the article treats these three phenomena as accidents rather than a direct consequence of the global connections

The Economist is celebrating. Its elegy to the old world fails to draw a clear line from connectivity to convergence to competition, and ultimately to conflict.

The more I've tried to understand our politics, the more I've become uneasy with the idea that we can ever resume progress towards 'one world'. Internationalists risk alienating the very people they need to persuade by implying they have 'closed' minds, or are ignorant and parochial. But more troublingly, the division between 'open' and 'closed' mindsets fails to capture the grand paradox shaping our times: *the more people and countries are drawn together, the more they want to be apart.* The core organizing principle of today's world is not a battle between globalists and nationalists over drawbridges, but rather a set of 'connectivity conflicts' that rages between interlinked antagonists. The act of linking people together does not always lead to conflict, but it can trigger reactions that make it more likely – as well as supplying the means for fighting.

Maybe it's because of a feeling that everything is changing that people have been so desperate for things to go back to 'normal', a restoration of more optimistic times. After Covid, Trump and Brexit it is not surprising that so many of us want life to be more boring, predictable, humdrum. But most of us feel in our bones that 'normality' is the one thing that will forever remain out of reach. Dramas that are meant to strike once a century seem to afflict us every few minutes. No sooner has one turned our world upside down, than another threatens to disrupt our lives once again.

I have often wondered what it would be like to write a book at a moment of world historic change – say in 1914, 1929, 1939 or 1945 – when history was out of joint and refused to follow the old rules. Would I understand that we were on the cusp of historical change? What would it be like to chronicle the world that was lost, to diagnose its downfall or sketch a blueprint for a different future? Our era shares a lot of the uncertainty of those earlier turning points, but it is different in one important respect. Each of those junctures gave rise to an awakening that would fundamentally change the way people lived and the ideas they believed in. The First World War buried empires and globalization. The Depression did the same to economic liberalism. The Second World War persuaded leaders to trade total war for cold war. But today we do not seem ready to give up on the things creating the most anguish in our interconnected world.

I wish that, like Woodrow Wilson, John Maynard Keynes, or Dean Acheson, we could conjure up a new architecture for a new world order. But, unlike in these earlier periods, I don't think this is a time for architects and master builders – after all no one wants to lose connectivity. And, in many ways, it is the grand plans of earlier architects of globalization which are coming back to haunt us.

Rather than architects, we need to find therapists who can help us accept who we are – and teach us to manage our demons. We have developed technologies which give us the power of gods. We are capable of solving so many of the problems that have blighted humanity in the past: hunger, disease, and a failure to understand different cultures.

But these same technologies are also capable of taking our world over the edge. The nightmare scenario is that we see a layering of connectivity attacks that fall short of war: catastrophic cyber attacks, trade wars that break down global supply chains, financial crises that plunge the world into depression. At the same time nationalist governments could manipulate climate change to hurt their rivals, driving waves of refugees from their homes, and spreading diseases around the world. With all of our advances in science and technology the one thing we have failed to understand is how our connected world is stoking envy while giving countries and people weapons to hurt one another.

It is not too late to change course. This is an argument for self-knowledge. Rather than treating our conflicts as external forces, we need to truly understand their origins in our lifestyle and choices (not just the big ones but the little decisions we are not even aware of having made). By analysing ourselves we can prepare for trouble and determine what choices we have left.

Our goal must be not to dispense with connectivity but to disarm it. We should try to remove the sting from interdependence or at least learn to coexist with powers motivated by values we do not share. There are some reasons to believe that this could happen. In China the government has embraced the idea of 'dual circulation' – an attempt to recalibrate its engagement with the world so that it feels less threatened by the world outside. In Washington, Joe Biden is reaching out to the people who felt they were the losers from our connected world – while rethinking America's trade, technology and foreign policies to make them less open to external manipulation. And in Europe the quest for European sovereignty and autonomy marks a shift from pulling down walls to making interdependence feel safe again.

There have been millions of words written on the contemporary crisis of politics. But very few commentators have confronted the fact that it's the very process of linking up the world that is leading to its division. This book tries to shed light on the big dilemma of our age: we can't go back to a world before connectivity, but humanity may not survive if we don't change our mindset. I show how connectivity creates the opportunity, the motive and the means for conflict. And I end by asking what kind of future we can build together (and which one we should avoid).

The biggest challenge during the Cold War was about controlling the spread of nuclear weapons before they ended humanity's existence. The challenge of our age is not to control the flow of weapons but to disarm connectivity itself.

The difference between an era of unprecedented opportunity and the collective suicide of humanity lies in the political choices we make over the next few years. The future is ours to shape.

PART ONE:

THE OPPORTUNITY

CHAPTER ONE:

THE GREAT CONVERGENCE

On my first trip to China everything was bewildering. The unfamiliar tones of the language, traffic jams that stretched to eternity, a shadowy political system, and numbers that were too big for my brain to grasp. I remember spending hours in big ceremonial chairs, drinking tea and exchanging formal small talk with officials, with no idea where our conversations were leading. But most unsettling of all was the gulf between how my Chinese interlocutors saw their country's future and the way it was understood in Europe and America. Over the next two decades – during dozens more visits and time spent as a fellow at the Chinese Academy of Social Sciences in Beijing – what had seemed strange became familiar and understandable. I got used to the language, the congestion, the pollution, the etiquette and made friends with many people who had initially greeted me with stiff formality. But the one thing I never came to terms with was the gap in perceptions between East and West.

Western diplomats and journalists consistently told me China was coming round to their ways of working. As it was integrated into the global system, Beijing would become a custodian of a global order which had allowed it to lift hundreds of millions of people out of poverty in a single generation. As China's middle class grew, its members would demand cleaner air, less corrupt courts and eventually liberal democracy. China would become like us – or it would fail. But because failure was not an option, it would become like us. The eventual pay-off would be global peace and harmony. There was only one problem with this scenario: the Chinese.

The thinkers and officials I talked to saw things differently. They were curious and had a magpie instinct to grab any ideas, technologies or concepts that would help their country prosper. But most wanted to emancipate their country from the West rather than slavishly follow its ideas. I met brilliant economists, political scientists, philosophers, military strategists and technologists, all thinking big thoughts about the future of their country. They effortlessly fused Western ideas with Beijing's socialist tradition and ancient Chinese wisdom. I became so fascinated that I spent years with them and their work and wrote two books about the development of a China model that could challenge the West. But of all the conversations I had on that first trip one really stood out, a discussion with a professor at the prestigious Tsinghua University called Yan Xuetong.

A smallish man with a square head, blow-dried spiky hair and rectangular glasses, Yan Xuetong would probably not stand out in a crowd. But in the cautious world of Chinese academia he has not been afraid to go against the grain. When China was trying to keep a low profile and maintain friendly relations with America, he called on Beijing to be more assertive and to toughen diplomacy with Washington and its allies in Taiwan and Japan. When Chinese leaders contrasted their country's non-alignment with Washington's 'cold war' institutions such as NATO, he called on Beijing to develop rival alliances to reduce its international isolation. At a time when most scholars were translating Western texts and denying the existence of a 'China model', he launched a quest to develop a 'Chinese School' of international relations. And while Beijing was trying to stress its economic importance and downplay its political and military role, he set up a big international conference on China's role in international security, persuading then Vice President Xi Jinping to make his first big foreign policy speech there.[1] When he called his conference on political power the 'World Peace Forum', I remember thinking that I had never heard the word 'peace' used in such an aggressive way! Back in 2002, when I first met him, Yan Xuetong was characteristically assertive. I had spent days talking to European diplomats and Chinese officials about what China wanted from Europe. Everyone spoke blandly about 'win-win' economic development and cooperation on global problems, but Professor Yan had a more specific demand: 'When China goes to war with the USA,' he said in a matter-of-fact voice, 'we hope Europe will at least stay neutral.'

I still remember the shock of hearing him utter those words: 'When', not 'if', we go to war. Yan's words were delivered in a soothing voice but they went through me like an electric shock. My friends in Washington and Brussels hoped that binding China into the global system through burgeoning trade and supply chains had made war irrational. They thought that opening institutions like the World Trade Organization to China would persuade it that it had a stake in the existing order. And they hoped the internet would erode remaining political differences. Speaking at an event in March 2000, US President Bill Clinton summed up the prevailing thinking: 'The Beijing regime has been trying to crack down on the internet,' he said. 'Good luck! That's sort of like trying to nail jello to the wall.'

But here was Yan Xuetong talking about war. And what's more – like many of the other thinkers I spoke to – he had not given up on the idea of nailing jello to the wall. Professor Yan likes to frame complex ideas in readily graspable terms. In his writing he has used a famous fairy tale – one that every Chinese child learns at primary school – to explain the problems Beijing will encounter if it tries to mimic the West. The story, known as *dong shi xiao pin*, is about two women, a rare beauty named Xishi (whose name means West) and an unusually ugly woman called Dongshi (whose name means East). Xishi, one of the 'four beauties' of ancient China, suffered from a congenital heart condition that made her wince with pain. When she wrinkled her forehead she would become even more beautiful than normal. Dongshi would imitate her and crinkle her forehead in a similar way. However, the more she tried to emulate the beauty, the uglier she would become. The moral of the story: don't blindly imitate others. What works for them may not work for you. And Yan's fairy tale was very much in line with what I picked up from economists, political scientists, philosophers and other licensed free-thinkers in Chinese think-tanks, universities and party organs.

Two decades on from our first encounter Yan Xuetong's fighting words have lost their outlandish quality. As tensions between China and the United States ramp up, the language of conflict is more common than talk of global peace. And the big question in many European countries is precisely the one Yan Xuetong had originally posed: whether to align with America, or try to stay neutral. Many people fear the world might once again collapse into conflicts more resonant of twentieth-century divisions than twenty-first-century millennial visions of digital harmony.

Some have compared China's challenge to Germany in 1914 or 1939 but the most popular analogy is with the contest with the Soviet Union during the Cold War. However we are not in a Cold War 2.0. There is no iron curtain separating China from America – and the tensions between the two sides are a product of their connections rather than their separation. In fact, for most of the last thirty years there was an almost perfect symbiosis between Beijing and Washington DC. Chinese savings bank-rolled American consumption; China's manufacturing workhouse made products designed and serviced by America's post-industrial economy;

and its introverted foreign policy did not fundamentally undermine Washington's global leadership. The USA was the leader of the developed world while China was the biggest developing country. In fact, China and America were bound so closely together that some analysts came up with a compound name to describe the phenomenon: 'Chimerica'.[2] It's not just that China exports vast amounts to the USA or that key sectors of the US economy – from Apple smartphones to soybeans – rely heavily on Chinese markets.[3] The financial relationship was worth over $5 trillion in 2019, including nearly $2 trillion in Chinese listings on US stock exchanges and $1.3 trillion in Chinese official holdings of US government bonds.[4] Chimerica was possible because the governing philosophies on either side of the Pacific mirrored each other so perfectly – so much so that they came to depend upon each other.

Of course, during this period there was competition as well as cooperation between China and the US. But because they were starting from such different places, any contradictions between the two systems were manageable. In Asia, the USA concentrated on military primacy and had bilateral links to its allies, while resisting non-US-led economic initiatives. In contrast, China sought to reassure its neighbours by supporting multilateral regional integration and giving them an economic stake in China's rise through trade deals. While the USA focused on its relations with advanced democracies and energy-rich countries in the Middle East, China put much of its diplomatic activism into its immediate neighbours as well as increasing its presence in the neglected regions of Africa and Latin America.

But since the financial crisis in 2008, the post-Cold War consensus in both America and China has increasingly been questioned – as have the prospects for a harmonious relationship between Washington and Beijing. The biggest driver of tensions is a shift in the balance of power between the two countries. When China joined the World Trade Organization in 2001 (with assistance from the USA), its economy was just over a tenth of the size of America's. By 2019, China's economy was over two-thirds the size of America's.[5] This economic shift also transformed the two countries' relations with other players. In 2001, more than 80 per cent of countries traded more with the USA than with China. By 2018, only 30 per cent did, while 128 out of 190 countries traded more with China than with the United States.[6]

Since the Peloponnesian Wars strategists have been alert to the tensions between rising and declining powers. But these tensions seem to have been accentuated by the way that the USA and China have mirrored each other as part of their spiralling competition. The best place to see them becoming more similar – and thus more competitive – is in the realm of technology, the fiercest battleground in their emerging competition. Although a war over Taiwan or an atoll in the South China Sea is frighteningly possible, the main conflicts of our age of unpeace are different from those that Yan Xuetong conjured at the turn of the century. The front line is as much in the infrastructure of our connected world as in the land, air or sea.

The burgeoning digital connections that Clinton saw as the key to harmony seem to have created the biggest tensions between China and America. Rather than making geopolitical competition irrational, it seems that connectivity is making it almost inevitable. The technologies that promised peace in fact increase the opportunity for conflict. They open up new battlegrounds and supply ever more reasons for resentment and fear. To discover why, you need only travel a few blocks from the office where I met Yan Xuetong on my first trip to China.

SENSETIME AND FACEBOOK

On the fringes of the sprawling campus of Tsinghua University in Beijing's university district are the gleaming 'Science Park Towers'. These four phallic protrusions shoot over 100 metres into the air and frame a pedestrian square with a monumental bronze sculpture of two bulls in the centre. Innovation Plaza, as it's called, has become a space for young Chinese people to hang out, drink coffee and socialize. When I was last there, a group of teenage girls was practising a dance routine in the shadow of the buildings.

SenseTime's Beijing office is in Tower B. When I entered the reception I was greeted with examples of the company's world-beating facial recognition software in action. One screen captured my face and described my gender, age, wardrobe, how attractive and happy I am; and the kind of marketing information to which I might be susceptible. In my case, I was flattered to be told that I was thirty-four years old (I was forty-four), have 93 attractiveness points and am 91 per cent happy. The machine told me that I was the second most attractive person in the building (I never found out who the most attractive person was) and that I had a special affection for the director Christopher Nolan. The findings were not correct in every regard, but the fact that it made them with such confidence was impressive (although it is unnerving to think that such inaccurate tools are being used to judge people). It was a symbol of the way algorithms and big data are deployed to create model consumers and citizens in China – just like in the West.

Tsinghua's Science Park is not quite Palo Alto or even Shenzhen: the toilets are in a state of disrepair, and staff sit cheek by jowl in over-crowded open-plan offices or tiny windowless cubicles. But just like in Silicon Valley, the air crackles with ideas and ambition. The woman who showed me around was called June Jin. Like many Chinese execs, she was headhunted from Microsoft. SenseTime's founder appointed her Chief Marketing Officer when he transformed the organization from an academic project into a business. Her mission was to think about how to position SenseTime as it went from being a small start-up to a global titan. In the year after she joined, the staff grew from 700 to 1,700. The founders used three rounds of investment to raise over $2 billion, sending its value to almost $8 billion and making it the most valuable artificial intelligence company in the world. Its list of backers includes China's Alibaba, Singapore's Temasek, UK-based Fidelity International, and US chipmaker Qualcomm.[7] June explains that the staff is filled with 'ex-Microsofties' such as the MD and the head of engineering, as well as June Jin herself. Like Microsoft, SenseTime has a way of blending corporate and academic cultures. Most founders have PhDs. 'When I joined SenseTime,' June told me, 'none of my friends or family really understood what we did. But then two big things happened. First DeepMind's AlphaGo beat the world champion at Go. Then Xi Jinping published the "next generation AI" strategy which declared it a national priority. This allowed our funding to take off.'

There weren't many people in the West who noticed when the AlphaGo computer beat Lee Sedol, the world champion, at Go (a Chinese precusor to chess) in 2016. But the Chinese did. Almost 300 million of them tuned in to watch the five-match contest and witness the moment when artificial intelligence overtook human brainpower. Lee Sedol had been as dominant in his sport as Roger Federer was in tennis or Lionel Messi in football. But during the course of five games he found himself out-manoeuvred, out-thought and ultimately outplayed by an algorithm. And, to add to the humiliation from Beijing's perspective, the computer that had mastered the game invented in ancient China 2,500 years ago was made in Britain. AlphaGo – the algorithm developed by the AI start-up DeepMind which had been acquired a few years earlier by Google – was turning the natural order on its head.

The Asian investor Kai-Fu Lee has called this a 'Sputnik moment' for China, evoking the deep anxiety felt by Washington in October 1957 when the Soviet Union launched the first human-made satellite into orbit. Americans were so traumatized by this event that they invested billions in maths and science education and research and did not rest

until they had put a man on the moon and developed a series of technologies from supersonic rockets to missile shields. One by-product of
this orgy of innovation was the creation of the internet by a little-known
research agency funded by the Department of Defense, DARPA. In
other words, Sputnik did not simply launch a space race, it spurred decades of innovation. Paradoxically the ultimate beneficiary of this process
was not the Soviet Union that launched the race, but rather the United
States that ended up winning it.

Kai-Fu Lee predicts that the race to develop artificial intelligence
could follow a similar trajectory. Although it was a Western algorithm
that first managed to beat the world champion at Go, it is China that
could eventually win the race. It is certainly true that when China had
its Sputnik moment, it aimed for the stars. When President Xi Jinping
launched the white paper June Jin mentioned, in 2017, he called for
China to get into the first tier of AI powers by 2020, and to lead the
world by 2030. In China when the emperor – or general secretary of the
Communist Party – launches a national goal like this it reverberates
through the system and is reflected in the priorities and decisions of
every province, municipality, city, town, village as well as the party com-
mittees of all major corporations and banks. In addition to the billions
Xi Jinping pledged out of the federal budget, his national plan opened
the way for resources to cascade through the system at all levels of government and in the private sector too. And his digital silk road promised
to help Chinese AI find a global market for its products. The national
plan also makes data available to Chinese researchers and companies,
something which China's surveillance state has in abundance. Where
most Western companies were working with a database of just 13 million faces, SenseTime claims to have access to over 2 billion faces to
train their algorithms on.[8]

Xi Jinping set his government on a quest to recruit talent by introducing tax breaks and other incentives for Chinese researchers who

return to the motherland. In 2014 Tsinghua was the only Chinese university in a ranking of the top fifteen whose researchers were presenting papers at prestigious artificial intelligence conferences. Although China was still behind the USA in leagues of the most influential researchers, by 2018 there were four Chinese institutions in the top fifteen and Tsinghua maintained its place as number two in the world, well ahead of Silicon Valley's Stanford University.[9] Maybe the key driver of success in AI is the corporate ecosystem. And by 2020, there was a vibrant mix of private technology giants (Alibaba, Tencent, Baidu, Huawei and Xiaomi) that rivalled the American giants in their customer base and turnover. These have been joined by large investors and venture capitalists from the private sector as well as the state. Maybe most surprising are the start-ups that are finding global markets with world-beating technologies. And one of the best examples of that new breed of company is SenseTime.

With the slogan 'AI for a better tomorrow', SenseTime promises nothing less than to 'redefine human life as we know it'.[10] It all started in a much more modest way in 2014 as an academic project in the media lab at the University of Hong Kong, where professor Tang Xiao'ou worked with eleven of his students to develop an algorithm that identified faces with 98.52 per cent accuracy. Their results were better than all the other algorithms in the world. In fact, they were the first to be even more reliable than the human eye. Professor Tang still beams with pride at the achievement. Not only had his group of researchers made history, but even more importantly, they did it before the USA. 'We beat Facebook to the punch', he said in a speech at the Massachusetts Institute of Technology, where he had earned his PhD.[11] A year later the team spun off SenseTime as a business and one of the students – Xu Li – was appointed CEO.

SenseTime is not yet a household name but many Chinese consumers will come across it several times every day. During the Covid-19 epidemic it developed a system for screening people in subway stations and public places, scanning passengers from a distance and identifying individuals with a fever and cross-referencing their faces against a database of identity cards.[12] Its technology allows people to unlock their mobile phones, pay for subway tickets, open their bank accounts, pass a credit check and carry out a host of other tasks through facial recognition. SenseTime offers software to apps like Meitu, Weibo and handset-makers like Xiaomi and Oppo to improve photo-sorting or image editing.[13] It works with peer-to-peer lending companies to identify prospective clients online. It helps universities measure the attendance of their students. And, most intriguingly, it limits the use of toilet paper in Beijing's Temple of Heaven (it scans people's faces and restricts each person to 60 cm of paper every nine minutes). SenseTime has signed contracts with 127 cities in China to help them with everything from traffic management to crowd control.[14]

SenseTime is not just changing the Chinese way of life. The firm has global ambitions. It has announced plans for an R&D hub in Abu Dhabi. It launched a 'smart health' lab in the USA to use AI for diagnosing cancer. It set up an autonomous driving test centre in Japan with Honda Motors. And it is helping Malaysia build a $1 billion 'AI Park' to develop robots that can process images, human speech and different languages. What is more, it earned the government's seal of approval when it was picked for its 'AI National Team' alongside the Chinese internet titans of Baidu, Alibaba and Tencent.[15] Since 2015, SenseTime's research team has presented more new studies at the world's major AI conferences than Google or Facebook.[16] The company's Chinese name is Shang-Tang, after the first Chinese dynasty Shang (eighteenth to eleventh century BC) and its first emperor, Tang. The founder Tang Xiao'ou explained his thinking: 'That was a time when China led the world and it will again with its technological innovations.'[17] Many Westerners fear he is right. Eric Schmidt, the former chair of Google, has warned that

China 'will have caught up with us by 2025. And by 2030 they will dominate the industry'.[18] Right on track.

In some ways SenseTime epitomizes the dreams of liberal globalists such as Bill Clinton at the turn of the century: that China would embrace new technologies; grow a capitalist middle class; and become a globally connected state. Today China has more internet users than the United States. Its middle class is larger than the USA's entire population. It has overtaken the West to become the first cashless society. And the internet, through platforms like WeChat and Weibo, has given Chinese citizens a noisy public sphere where they can congregate and debate (albeit with censorship on topics the government considers sensitive). What's more, this middle class is increasingly connected to the world. In 2017, Chinese outbound tourists took approximately 131 million trips, a figure that carried on growing until the onset of Covid-19. In 2018, there were more than 650,000 Chinese students studying overseas.[19]

But despite these developments, China hasn't followed the script written by the techno-utopians. They hoped that China's Communist Party would be swept aside by the internet. Instead, the party has used the web to strengthen its grip and now seeks to transform it. Censorship began in a tentative way in the 1990s when Bill Clinton was still president of the USA, but it gathered pace in the early years of this century as the government began to restrict access to foreign companies with what came to be known as the 'Great Firewall'. While millions of Chinese people can stay in Hilton and Hyatt hotels, wake up with a Starbucks, gorge themselves on Kentucky Fried Chicken or McDonald's, wear Nike trainers and drink Coke, they are not allowed to use Google, Amazon, Facebook or Twitter.

From the nineteenth century onwards, China has had an ambivalent relationship with Western technology. It recognizes that it needs it to develop but is scared about changing the essence of China, and determined to avoid the humiliation and coercion it suffered at the hands of the British and French in past centuries. In the early days of the internet, the government tried to find a modus vivendi by allowing companies like Microsoft and Google into China but demanding that they abide by local censorship laws and provide access to information about their users. But after a game of cat and mouse, it would in effect block Silicon Valley's tech platforms from China's online life. This opened up a space for entrepreneurs to develop Chinese alternatives to the American platforms that would be under greater control by the Communist Party. The government could insist that all the servers be based in Beijing and ensure that executives obeyed the Communist Party's strictures. As a result the search engine Baidu mirrored Google; the e-commerce company Alibaba stood in for eBay and Amazon; WeChat for WhatsApp; Weibo for Twitter; and Didi Chuxing for Uber. They are not just carbon copies but are developing new ways of serving the consumer within China's controlled political and economic system.

A semi-controlled public sphere emerged with a flourishing of debate and accountability on platforms like Weibo and WeChat. The authorities in Beijing did not feel threatened because they could employ armies of tens of thousands of censors to remove material that spelled political trouble. The information they gleaned from social media allowed them to spot and address any sources of discontent. Even the exposure of the corruption of local party officials was seen as useful – allowing central authorities to deflect discontent on to 'bad eggs' rather than bringing the whole system into question. Ultimately, because the servers were based in Beijing the authorities could always track down any internet 'troublemakers' and arrest or imprison them.

Then in 2011 a demonstrator set himself on fire in a second-tier Tunisian town and lit a spark of protest that spread across the Middle East on Twitter and Facebook. The Communist Party immediately became more anxious about social media. When Xi Jinping became president in 2012 he appointed a new internet tsar who was charged with making online China safe for one-party rule. Lu Wei, the charismatic head of the Central Leading Group for Cyberspace Affairs, set about dismantling the three features of the internet that the Chinese authorities credited with spreading revolution: anonymity, virality and impunity.[20] First, he introduced rules making it compulsory for Chinese netizens to register their real names and phone numbers, making it much easier for authorities to locate the authors of individual posts. Next he set about expanding and outsourcing censorship to make sure that politically sensitive material would not have the chance to go viral. Rather than assembling a massive bureaucracy itself, the state tasked all the leading private internet platforms with censoring their own sites in line with the government's guidelines. As a result each of the Chinese internet giants recruited tens of thousands of censors to keep an eye on their websites. I remember that around that time a friend who worked for the search engine Baidu explained to me how the company tried to enhance the consumer experience by market testing the ways people most liked being censored. He told me users are happier if they are allowed to make a post – even if it is taken down immediately – than being stopped from putting it up in the first place. Finally Lu Wei tried to raise the stakes for potential troublemakers. In 2013 the authorities launched a campaign against 'online rumours' that saw a number of celebrity bloggers arrested and shamed on national television. By 2015 the Chinese police had arrested over 15,000 people for so-called 'internet crimes', which covered all content that the Communist Party deemed unhelpful.

If the first wave of the Chinese internet was mostly about replicating the success of Western companies in a protected home market, the next wave of Chinese tech has been more about innovation than imitation. Many Chinese companies now set the pace for global development – one that's taking us away from freedom and openness.

The SenseTime headquarters is the perfect place to see this in action. Alongside demonstrations of virtual reality games and self-beautifying selfie apps, SenseTime showcases the technology of Beijing's nascent surveillance state. One module shows CCTV cameras capturing cars on roads and people on the street. Algorithms zone in on the conduct of individuals and groups to spot suspicious behaviour. The technology is engrossing and disturbing in equal measure. A rival firm had an even more dramatic demo. It played footage of the 2013 Boston Marathon bombing – and sought to show that if the US authorities had been using their technology they would have discovered the terrorists sufficiently quickly to arrest them before they executed their murderous plans. This shows that 'pre-crime prevention' is no longer a fantasy in Spielberg movies, it is part of everyday life in China.

People estimate there could be as many as 600 million surveillance cameras in China, and many public authorities installed more during the Covid crisis. SenseTime is creating five supercomputers to run the 'Viper' system it has developed to monitor their images (their goal is to make sure they can automatically analyse the feeds of up to 100,000 cameras at a time).[21]

The surveillance technologies pioneered by start-ups like SenseTime have been tested in the majority-Muslim region of Xinjiang, which the Beijing authorities fear could become a hotbed of Islamic extremism and secessionism. Pervasive cameras scan the population, and algorithms are trained to spot the difference between the 11 million Muslims and the non-Muslim population. According to a report in the *New York Times*, SenseTime's technology has been used to create a vast surveillance net, deploying artificial intelligence to facilitate this racial profiling.[22] The technology has been used to store and analyse information on the DNA, number plates, social media activity, religious activities, friendships and movements of the population.[23] A recent data leak suggests that police have generated lists of 'untrustworthy' people based on criteria such as having relatives abroad, wearing traditional Islamic clothing or having submitted petitions to the government.[24]

Such lists are then used to select people to stop and search or interrogate at numerous police checkpoints in the region's cities and on its roads.

In a series of brutal crackdowns with names such as the 'Strike Hard Campaign' the government has rounded up and detained over a million citizens in camps where they face indoctrination, forced labour and even sterilisation.[25] Faced with international criticism, Beijing tried to pass the camps off as 'vocational training sites' but this did not convince NGOs like Human Rights Watch or the United Nations Human Rights Council who have condemned the practice of arbitrary mass detention. These camera technologies have also been used in Hong Kong, newly under China's direct rule, which is why protesters started to wear black masks to avoid recognition.

Another experiment in surveillance technology is taking place in Rongcheng, a town in Shandong province, where one of the first so-called 'social credit' schemes began in 2015.[26] 'Social credit' is an attempt to gather all the data possible about Chinese inhabitants and to give them a single score which shows whether they are a good or bad citizen. Under this scheme, all citizens receive a score up to a maximum of 900 points. If they cross the street when there is a red light, they lose 20 points and their face is displayed on a giant screen; other misdemeanours – such as being active in societies that protect workers, calling for collective bargaining; or being friends with known 'trouble-makers' – could also cost points. The ultimate goal of the new technology is to use artificial intelligence and big data to spot anti-government activity, disturbances and crimes *before* they happen.

The connections between China and America have led to a great deal of fear and uncertainty on the Chinese side – a horror that they might open the system to challenge or blackmail. That is why they talk about the possibility of the Chinese and American economies 'decoupling'. But on the internet, decoupling is already well under way. It started when China effectively blocked Western platforms in order to build a parallel online space. As a result the internet which was meant to knit the world together is actually balkanizing itself. China's push towards authoritarian technology has, it is claimed by leading technologists such as ex-Google chairman Eric Schmidt, led to the age of the 'splinternet'. He claims that the digital world is dividing in two, much as the analogue world did during the Cold War. Instead of the free world and the Soviet Union, they claim, we now have a Chinese internet and an open one. For SenseTime this became real when it was added to a blacklist by the US Department of Commerce in October 2019 in connection with human rights violations against Uyghurs and other members of Muslim minority groups in Xinjiang.[27] It may have had plans for global expansion but it is now banned from working with institutions like MIT (where its founder received his PhD) as well as companies like Microsoft (where so many of its leading lights started their careers). In the long run this decoupling may soothe tensions between the two countries, but the way it is being pursued now is adding to the mutual insecurity, and fuelling talk of a new cold war.

One of the most eloquent denunciations of the Chinese internet was delivered by the CEO of Facebook, Mark Zuckerberg, in a speech to Georgetown University in 2019. Dressed informally in a trademark black sweatshirt he walked up to an imposing wooden lectern in an oak-panelled auditorium. He started by saying that Facebook has two driving ambitions: to connect the world and to give people a voice. Beijing, he argued, is the biggest threat to both. 'China is building its own internet focused on very different values,' he exclaimed, 'and is now exporting their vision of the internet to other countries.' A decade ago, he explained, almost all of the major internet platforms were American. Today, he bemoaned, six of the top ten are Chinese. 'Is that the internet we want?' he asked.

Zuckerberg's speech was particularly striking because he has worked harder than any other American tech leader to woo the Chinese political leadership. In 2014 Mark Zuckerberg organized a personal tour of the Facebook headquarters – in Mandarin – for Lu Wei, the face of censorship in China. He even allowed Lu Wei to sit at his desk, which was adorned with a bound copy of the collected speeches of the Chinese President Xi Jinping. 'I bought this book for my colleagues,' Zuckerberg said, 'I wanted them to understand socialism with Chinese characteristics.' In 2015, Zuckerberg showed off his Mandarin once again when he met President Xi Jinping at the White House. He asked the leader of the Chinese Communist Party to give his unborn child an honorary Chinese name (Xi Jinping declined on the grounds that it was too great a responsibility). Later in the year, Zuckerberg made yet another attempt to ingratiate himself. He headed to Yan Xuetong's alma mater, Tsinghua University, where he gave a twenty-minute speech in Mandarin.

Why did Zuckerberg have such a change of heart? Was it a recognition that his campaign to break into the Chinese market would never succeed? Was it to curry favour with an American political class that is souring on China? Or could it be an attempt to deflect criticism of Facebook's unscrupulous use of surveillance and data by presenting China as an even bigger threat to our liberties? In any case it is interesting that even as he changed his public tone on the moral value of the Chinese internet, many of his colleagues were privately trying to mimic the business models adopted by China's internet giants such as WeChat and TikTok.[28] In many ways the West is becoming more Chinese (as we will explore later). Personally, I first understood how China and America are converging in the extractive way they use data when visiting Facebook's headquarters in Palo Alto. I discovered why the fears people hold about China's 'surveillance state' have their mirror image in those expressed about America's 'surveillance capitalism'. This was a strange cycle. We first thought the internet would bring us together. The Chinese worried about it changing them and strove for decoupling. But now that their companies have been so successful, it is the West that is in the mimicking business and this convergence is creating a new opportunity for conflict.

I visited the Facebook campus for the first time in 2017 when employees still beamed with pride at the utopian community of which they were part. They took me around restaurants, juice bars, bike shops, woodcutting and poster shops, machines that vended Apple products, laundromats and yoga studios. It was consumer heaven, but all the outlets had a twist: they didn't accept money from Facebook employees. Everything was free! I couldn't help thinking that here, goods flowed from each according to their ability to each according to their need.

My guide took me to a roof garden on top of one of the office blocks where hummingbirds flitted around newly installed trees, grasses and flowers. Free concerts from famous bands were held in the summer and, every Friday, there was a town hall meeting with the Facebook leadership. Next, my guide showed me the largest open-plan office in the world, designed by Frank Gehry no less, which embodied Facebook's commitment to transparency and even featured a 'newsfeed' wall. He told me about the 'faciversaries' for all members of staff and the boot camp and induction courses at which they are onboarded when they start work. 'Don't be an asshole', was apparently the most important lesson. I was blown away both by the opulence and by the egalitarian ethos. As I spent longer there I tried to think about what it reminded me of. Eventually I came to a surprising conclusion. The culture of the Facebook headquarters in Menlo Park reminded me more than anything else of the histories I had read of the professed goals of the Chinese Communist Party in the Mao era. With its slogans pasted on the walls; its determination to combine work and play; its lofty idealism; its appeals to youth and its attempts to socialize people into something bigger than themselves, it echoed many of the ideals of the party's founders. How strange that China's new entrepreneurs that I met in Beijing seemed far more like cut-throat capitalists than the utopian socialists of Facebook's headquarters.

When I returned to Facebook in late 2019, a few months before the outbreak of Covid-19, the atmosphere was somewhat more muted. Rather than lecturing others about their behaviour, Facebook staff were being attacked over their own practices. From Cambridge Analytica and fake news to allegedly facilitating the genocide of the Rohingya and being accused of glamorizing suicide, Facebook found itself involved in daily news crises. The accusations came thick and fast: monopolistic practices; the manipulation of reality through algorithms that select and order information; disrespect for privacy; emotional, racial and personality profiling; meddling in elections and tax evasion to name just a few. Underlying it all was a charge that the company had put its pursuit of profit above all else. It had transformed itself from a social networking site with a mission to connect the world into an advertising behemoth that would extract as much money as possible from selling the attention of its users.

Shoshana Zuboff's path-breaking work on 'surveillance capitalism' strips away the illusion that the internet is about spreading freedom, 'that being connected', as she puts it, 'is somehow intrinsically pro-social, innately inclusive, or naturally tending towards the democratization of knowledge'.[29] Instead she revives Marx's idea of capitalism as a vampire that feeds on labour, except in the internet age it is human experience which is being fed on rather than labour. Companies such as Google and Facebook have found ways of using our search histories, our likes and dislikes, our messages and even our movements to work out how to grab our attention, offering clients the chance to nudge and manipulate our behaviour in exchange for a fee.

Facebook's powerful attention-seeking algorithms were accused of nothing less than destroying free will, by redefining reality and depriving citizens of the chance to make real informed choices. As a result of all this criticism, Facebook announced a major reset of its approach. Zuckerberg agreed to give evidence to lawmakers and patiently submitted himself to questions from Congress and the European Parliament (although he refused to appear in the UK). Facebook drafted in the former UK Deputy Prime Minister Nick Clegg as its new public policy tsar. It went from opposing regulation to asking legislators to set standards for tech platforms to follow. And, in a strange twist, it uses the same technique that Chinese companies have used to reassure the authorities by recruiting an army of 35,000 'security staff' to police the web. They set about deleting fake accounts and taking down offensive posts, at an annual cost roughly equivalent to Facebook's entire turnover when the company was listed on the stock exchange in 2012.[30]

What is more, my Chinese friends like to point out that long before China developed its surveillance techniques in Xinjiang Western intelligence agencies were capturing big data to fight their own 'global war on terror'. The whistleblower Edward Snowden's revelations showed almost a decade ago how the surveillance state and surveillance capitalism can end up working together to erode individual freedom.[31] His leaked documents in 2013 revealed the existence of a global surveillance apparatus run by the United States' National Security Agency that was secretly accessing Yahoo! and Google data centres to collect information from hundreds of millions of account holders worldwide.[32] Snowden famously claimed that while working for the NSA, 'I, sitting at my desk [could] wiretap anyone, from you or your accountant, to a federal judge or even the president, if I had a personal email.'[33] One of the slides he leaked showed that the NSA's stated objective was to 'Collect it All', 'Process it All', 'Exploit it All', 'Partner it All', 'Sniff it All' and 'Know it All'.[34] More recently, the American Civil Liberties Union has warned of a 'land rush' in which companies and government agencies deploy new privacy-invasive technologies before subjects are aware that they exist – and certainly before we have consented to their use through our democratic political system.[35]

Nevertheless, it would be an absurd stretch to draw an equivalence between surveillance capitalism in the USA and the surveillance state in China. The unregulated use of data by private companies (that have, after Snowden, made it considerably harder for governments to access their products) and the unrestrained surveillance of an authoritarian state are distinct problems, even if they use similar technological tools. For the foreseeable future there will continue to be continent-sized differences between the vibrant democracy of the USA and the digital dictatorship of the People's Republic of China.

Binding two such different political systems together so tightly in a single economy has no doubt created a lot of tension. But what is more surprising is that some of the biggest conflicts have been caused by the opposite dynamic: China and the US becoming more alike.

IMITATION AND COMPETITION

It is maybe no coincidence that one of the people most conscious of the dangers of globalization is Peter Thiel, one of the architects of our hyper-connected world. Thiel was involved in developing the global payments system PayPal; pioneering big data through Palantir; and transforming people's social lives by backing companies like LinkedIn and Facebook, on whose board he still serves. I first met him in the UK in 2017, when I was invited to participate in a retreat of political and technology leaders he was chairing on the 'Future of the West'. We then carried on the conversation about globalization when I visited him in his native California.

Thiel is an intellectually restless contrarian who stunned many of his peers in 2016 by supporting Donald Trump in the presidential election. His biggest obsession is with the danger inherent in *imitation*, an interest he developed as an undergraduate at Stanford, while attending the classes of the French philosopher René Girard.

Girard turned the study of imitation into an art form. Known as the 'prophet of envy', he thought that humans' ability to copy each other was the characteristic that most differentiated us from other animals. Imitation, he reasoned, allows us to learn, to develop languages, religions, and craft our identities and cultures. But even more importantly, for Girard, imitation explains our *desires*. He rejected the romantic idea that our desires spring from deep inside our souls, a product of our 'inner', subjective preferences. Instead, he argued, our desires are 'mimetic', by which he meant they're copied from others, either consciously or unconsciously. For Girard, we imitate the desires of others to such a degree that the *object* of our desires often becomes secondary, and in some cases superfluous, to the rivalries that form around it.

Girard showed that as rivals compete for *any* desired object, each becomes ever more obsessed with the other. They mirror each other in order to win the object they seek. The irony is that as the rivalry intensifies, the mirroring process ends up eroding all the characteristics that previously distinguished one from the other. Eventually, the antagonists become 'doubles' of each other.

Girard's great insight is that rivalry in human relationships – between peoples and even between countries – is often rooted in *sameness* rather than *difference*. Imitation, he argues, eventually erases the differences between human beings, leading people who are similar to desire the same things. Conflicts between neighbours and nations are therefore often about what each has in common rather than what distinguishes one from the other. They go to war to prove they're different from an enemy who has become threateningly similar.[36]

In 2018, Peter Thiel agreed to co-teach a course on 'sovereignty and the limits of globalization and technology' at his alma mater, Stanford University.[37] Every Tuesday, 3.00–5.50 p.m., Thiel would gather with his co-professor Russell Berman to teach a hand-picked collection of students. 'The current historical moment appears to be marked by opposition to globalization', they wrote in the accompanying syllabus. 'This new mood is viewed as a break with a previous paradigm of international institutions and world citizenship.' The syllabus packs in a fascinating and eclectic selection of texts – from the Book of Genesis and *Hamlet* to the neo-conservative hero Leo Strauss and the former People's Liberation Army officer Liu Mingfu on the 'China Dream' to replace America. It gradually builds up to the pièce de résistance of the course, Thiel's intellectual hero René Girard. When they came to discuss Girard's work in class, Thiel claimed that China and the United States are increasingly becoming 'mimetic doubles' of each other. As they compete more strenuously to be the world's number one power, and mirror each other's strengths in order to advance that goal, they will inevitably become more and more alike – and their mutual antipathy will grow.[38]

Sigmund Freud argued that the process of becoming more alike creates a psychological need to seek out points of distinction, which he famously labelled the 'narcissism of small differences'.[39] Of course, states are not people with individual psychology, but they are governed by rulers and have citizens who do have these psychological features. And, as the distinction between foreign policy and domestic politics is eroded, these psychological factors matter ever more. Cultural traits that might seem intriguing when you have little contact can come to be seen as existential threats when you are bound together. If you take it down to the personal level, there are lots of examples of friends getting on very well until they become flatmates. The process of binding their lives together exposes different preferences, lifestyles and priorities. Rather than converting Beijing to supposedly universal norms, the West's policy of integration has exacerbated differences in some areas while making China and America converge in others.

THE CONNECTIVITY–SECURITY DILEMMA

The process of imitation and competition between two superpowers can take on a deadly quality. Security policy experts talk about the 'security dilemma' where insecure states build up their power to defend themselves from rivals. This in turn leads the other states to build up their own defences, thereby creating greater insecurity in their competitors and in the process setting off a vicious circle of insecurity and armament. The process of mirroring I described above shows that the security dilemma today applies as much to technology as it does to weapons.[40]

The United States is worried about 'economic aggression' from Beijing. Its officials fear losing technology through industrial espionage or forced technology transfers. They worry about American companies becoming uncompetitive in the face of China's state-subsidized national champions. They fear discriminatory regulations shutting them out of the Chinese market. And they worry that their open society is vulnerable to cyber attacks, fake news, espionage and political interference.

The American defence – tariffs, restrictions on inward investment, banning technology sales to certain Chinese companies, and indicting Chinese citizens and firms for espionage – is in turn stoking China's deepest vulnerabilities. Many Chinese officials and commentators do not see these moves as defensive. Instead they think that they are part of a containment strategy designed to stop China's economic and technological development. This in turn has led to Beijing's response of seeking greater self-reliance through its industrial policies to develop key technologies, big state subsidies for research, attempts to source new technology from abroad, and ever tighter links between the state and Chinese technology champions.

Why is it that technology has become so central to the conflict between China and America?

Military planners have taught us that conflict mirrors our society. As our economies moved from the industrial to the information age, so too did our military strategies. One of the big differences between the twenty-first century and the twentieth century is the flow of technology. In the last century many of the most advanced technologies – including the internet itself – migrated from the military to the civilian realm. But in the age of artificial intelligence, the most deadly technologies – from killer robots to cyber attacks – rely on know-how being developed in the private sector. Many tools with commercial applications can be redeployed as weapons. And so, to maintain its military edge over China, the USA needs to control the flow of technology.

Political economists will go even further, arguing that military and political power depends upon an economic foundation. The 'winner takes all' digital economy makes it imperative to be – and to remain – number one. There is a global race to define standards and norms and a fear that companies that come out on top will operate a scorched earth policy to wipe out their rivals. This is what American giants such as Microsoft, Google and Facebook stand accused of having done over the last two decades. They now fear that the next wave of monopolistic capitalism will have a Chinese face. And to make the competition less fair, these Chinese companies will benefit from state subsidies, a huge and protected home market, and political support from Beijing. The US government used to worry only about IP theft and illicit cyber attacks from Beijing, which ironically showed the strength of the US position. Now, the big fear is that China is competing on the same ground as the United States to become the global leader in new technologies such as 5G, artificial intelligence, quantum computing and blockchain (albeit 'unfairly' because of state support).

But the most fundamental reason lies in the way that technology is changing the nature of human interaction and, in doing so, changing our economies, societies, and politics. It was because they understood this that globalist leaders such as Bill Clinton were so keen to support the spread of the internet. They hoped that modems and mobile phones – the technologies of the 1990s – would bring freedom and individualism in their wake. This is also why the Chinese state was so keen to shut US technology platforms out of their country – even as they embraced Western car companies, Hollywood movies and even Western food brands.

China has sought for years to shut foreign companies out of its internet platforms and it is now trying to replace Western hardware with indigenous technology – for fear that Western companies might try to get involved in Chinese politics, refuse to hand over data to the government, be used to blackmail China or prevent home-grown companies from emerging.[41] But many Americans who once expected China to adopt American values now fear that their own country will be transformed by the Chinese Communist Party – or rather by the measures Washington feels it needs to take to defeat China or at least hold it at bay.

In August 2020, the US government launched its answer to the Chinese moves, the 'Clean Network' programme. Its goal is to ensure that all American telecoms networks, apps, app stores, cloud systems and undersea cables are 'clean' of any Chinese presence if they connect to American networks or transmit American data. The US government said that its 'Clean Network' programme would help protect business secrets while stopping the Chinese Communist Party from harvesting American citizens' data and thereby engaging in espionage, manipulation, and even political interference.[42] One congressional official was quoted explaining: 'We are finally having the debate China had two decades ago, when it found foreign technology threatening its political system. Only now is America catching up with foreign technology that is a direct threat to our open system.'[43] This effort to disentangle

American networks from Chinese ones has led regulators to scrutinize the security implications of Chinese investments. One of the most high-profile cases came with Grindr, the gay dating app which had been bought by Beijing Kunlun Tech, a gaming company. However, in March 2020, they announced they had been forced to sell Grindr to an American company after US regulators raised national security concerns.[44] There is now a real push to 'mirror China' (which in turn mirrored the US) through industrial policy, tariffs, export and import controls and subsidies. Increasingly, this requires the American government to get directly involved in the management of the US economy, as we saw through the dramatic events when the US government pressurized the Chinese company ByteDance to sell the video-sharing platform TikTok on national security grounds.[45]

For all the talk about freedom versus autocracy, the impact of technology on politics is not bifurcated. In some ways the connections between states accentuate political difference and cause tension. But because of the way they are mirroring each other to compete, networked technology is also blurring the comforting distinction between open and closed societies, planned and free economies – and ultimately making neither possible in its pure form. Seen from China, the digital age does not presage a battle between a liberal world and an authoritarian one, but the long-term convergence of the two. And many Americans are starting to fear the same thing. Yan Xuetong's fairy story now has resonance in Washington as well as Beijing. 'Are we now the ugly girl imitating the beauty?', Americans are starting to ask themselves, as their government adopts Chinese-style tactics from industrial planning and export controls to bans on investment and data-sharing. The more similar they become, the more conflict there is between Washington and Beijing not just in technological and economic terms, but in the military and political spheres too. Even on big global challenges that seem to threaten both superpowers equally – such as coronavirus and the climate crisis – the two giants have been inclined to fight rather than cooperate.

From trade and technology to migration and the internet, globalization itself is now being weaponized. In the fifth century it was possible for the Chinese fleet to cut across the Indian Ocean to India, the Arabian Peninsula and Africa without running into conflict with the West. But in our interconnected world it is almost impossible for China or America to sneeze without the other country catching a cold. Globalization provides both sides with many opportunities for competing with one another. In the next section of the book we will explore more deeply the *reasons* why these opportunities for competition are so often embraced, and the conflicts that they can produce within and between rival states.

The danger is that China and America are embarked on a deadly journey that sees connectivity lead to comparison, which in turn increases competition and conflict. The more competitive the relationship becomes, the greater the temptation to mimic one another, which in turn creates a vicious spiral of competition.

PART TWO:

THE REASONS

CHAPTER TWO:

CONNECTED MAN: HOW SOCIETY BECAME DIVIDED BY ENVY

There is a fine line between love and war, as any relationship counsellor can attest. And so it should maybe not have come as a surprise to Grindr, the world's largest gay dating app, when it found itself on the front line of the struggle between China and America.

Like all blossoming relationships the story began with high hopes, extravagant promises and grand plans when the Chinese gaming giant Beijing Kunlun bought a 60 per cent stake in the Hollywood-based company in 2016. Two years later it bought the remaining 40 per cent as part of its plan for global expansion for the network's almost 30 million users. But over time the relationship started to sour and doubts crept in on both sides. And in 2019 CFIUS, the American agency designed to investigate foreign takeovers, launched an investigation into the national security implications of the purchase and eventually ordered the two parties to split up.

What does a hook-up app have to do with national security, you may

ask? A lot, it seems, in this era of connected unpeace. The US government worried that a Chinese company might share sensitive information
about the location, sexual preferences and HIV status of millions of
Americans with the authorities in Beijing. They were particularly nervous about members of the armed forces or intelligence community
being open to blackmail. And so Beijing Kunlun was forced to sell up in
June 2020. But Grindr does not just tell us about the expanding zone of
tension between China and America; it also provides a window into
some of the ways that the digital revolution is changing our world, and
in the process giving people a reason to fight with one another. It
explains both the intoxicating attraction of connectivity and some of its
darker implications. Let's look at two of its users in different places.

Omar Abdulghani is one of Grindr's biggest fans. He doesn't just love
the internet – he reckons he was saved by it too. Born just outside
Damascus, he is one of the 11 million Syrians who fled their homes after
the country descended into murderous chaos in 2015. 'My phone helped
me with everything,' explained the twenty-year-old, as he described a
frightening odyssey which eventually took him to Amsterdam via Turkey, Greece and the Balkans.[1] Rather than relying on the unwieldy maps
or random acts of kindness that helped earlier generations of migrants,
Omar's passage was meticulously plotted online and executed through
his smartphone. It was not just his escape from Syria – every aspect of
his life has been shaped and improved by digital technology. As a gay
man, growing up in a country where homosexuality is still illegal, it
allowed him to explore his identity and meet friends and lovers. He
secretly found his first boyfriend through the gay dating app Grindr. As
the civil war threatened to tear the country apart, it was to the internet
that Omar turned for solace – sharing his growing fears and uneasiness
with friends he had met online. Eventually one sent him a plane ticket
to Istanbul as a birthday present. Once he reached Turkey he turned to
social networks and Grindr to 'couch-surf' his way to the Netherlands

where he lives today. The most perilous part of his journey was crossing the Aegean in a flimsy boat to Greece. He was only allowed a few treasured possessions, a small bag, a toothbrush, his tweezers and – most crucially – his phone. 'It felt like a horror movie,' he said. 'When we arrived at the beach, people got off and started kissing the ground. I was crying. I survived death. [. . .] Most of the other phones were dead because the water got in. But as for my phone, I put plastic wraps all over again and again and again.' It is no coincidence that Omar's phone was the object he took best care of as he set off across the sea. For him, it was not a luxury but a necessity – it is where his social life takes place, where he finds love and comfort from danger and how he finds his way around unknown cities. As for many in his generation, it is almost a physical extension of his being. The connections his device enables are central to his identity, whose very essence has been altered by hyper-connectivity. In many ways, Omar is an emblem of the new man shaped by hyper-connectivity.

Another user of Grindr who is part of the same generation is Matthieu Chartraire.[2] At the age of twenty-two, he was announced as the winner of the annual beauty contest in France's leading gay magazine, *Têtu*. He was the perfect pin-up: a rippling six-pack, great hair, beautiful eyes, a suggestive smile and a pensive look. But when his victory was announced it was another aspect of Matthieu's persona that attracted the most attention: his support for the far-right National Front. And once the initial shock in the national media had subsided it turned out that Matthieu is not alone. A poll by the firm IFOP in 2016 revealed that over a quarter of gay people in Paris supported the National Front as well. Like other far-right leaders such as Geert Wilders in the Netherlands, the National Front – now renamed the Rassemblement National – has made a point of using its antipathy to Islamism – and Islamism's homophobic supporters – as part of a recruiting drive in the LGBTQ community. Academics have even come up with a label for these kinds of voters:

'sexually modern nativists'.[3] They argue that the radical right is no longer the family of angry old men, but new identity groups who are uniting against a common enemy.

And so Grindr, Omar and Matthieu's favourite app, embodies many of the best and worst aspects of the connected world: it helps us understand why the three life-saving forces that shrink the world – global networks, emotional bonding, and effortless contact – also have digital doubles that make humans prone to conflict. In this chapter we will look at how connectivity is changing human nature and explore how the phenomena which connected Omar to the world are also leading to the polarization of society. We will look at how the emotional connections which allowed strangers to empathize with him are leading to an epidemic of envy. And we will see how the tech that made his social life and travel so effortless is making many people feel the world is out of control.

In all of these areas the technology of digital networks – restlessly exploited by surveillance capitalism – is driving societies apart and giving people a reason to fight with one another. Connected Man is increasingly susceptible to populist politics which in turn facilitate global disorder, as we will see in the next two chapters. To understand how the world is changing we need to begin with how human nature is being shaped by connectivity. We should look at the dark side of three of its most wonderful features.

INTEGRATION AND SEGREGATION

Older generations of gay men often faced a choice between either repressing their sexuality or risking exposure when frequenting gay bars or approaching strangers. But Omar and Matthieu were born into a world where dating apps make it possible to find other gay men and meet in private rather than public spaces (even in countries with repressive states). Sociologists have described hook-up apps as a kind of 'X-ray vision', allowing people to scan all the people in their vicinity, parsing the world into gay and straight inhabitants without anyone realizing.[4]

This is just part of the miracle of Grindr, which was launched in 2009 and created a community of tens of millions of people across 192 countries. It was the first app to combine online dating with geo-location. By giving people the option to swipe right and choose a mate it revolutionized the nature of courtship. It allows people who previously felt excluded and abnormal to be part of a community and has the potential to link people across ethnic and geographical boundaries. By connecting people across continents, it can broaden their empathetic horizons and allow gay people in London or Amsterdam to sympathize with their counterparts in Syria – as Omar happily discovered. Grindr provides a lifeline to the 35 per cent of the app's users who live in a country where it's illegal to be gay, as well as the millions who live in communities where it's still frowned upon.[5]

Nobody will complain about the fact that Grindr only brings gay people together. What would be the point of mixing gay and straight people in a dating app after all? And yet, people are becoming atomized. The very idea of a person is also being broken down into its component parts. On Grindr you can order prospective partners according to size, colour, body shape. Humans are sliced and diced into particular traits rather than treated as a whole.[6] People have come to think that they can pick out a partner in the same way they choose a car in a showroom or a yoghurt in a supermarket. Sociologists describe this as the 'consumerist illusion' because love's mysterious ways are different from other kinds of consumption.[7] A man can buy a particular brand of yoghurt without changing anything else in his life. It is much harder to contain the effects of one's choice of a life partner.

But after a few years, Grindr execs realized that they could make more money if they allowed people to look for prospective partners with even greater precision. In September 2013, to celebrate the fifth anniversary of the platform, they released version 2.0, which included a new filter allowing users to narrow their searches to help find their favourite 'Grindr Tribes': Bear (big and hairy – younger ones are called cubs); Daddy (over forty seeking younger man); Discreet (won't share photo/in the closet); Geek (glasses); Jock (muscular); Leather (S&M); Otter (hairy and slim); Poz (HIV positive); Rugged (highly masculine); Trans (transgender) and Twink (shaved or waxed, young and camp).[8]

On the surface this also looks like a great innovation. After all, isn't the point of a hook-up app to help people to find their 'type'? And the beauty of the internet is that everyone can be connected to everyone else – allowing users to massively increase their pool of possible contacts. Within this greater universe it is much more likely that everyone can find someone who matches their niche interests. And so it proved with Grindr.

The Grindr app was so popular among gay people that it was soon copied widely within the community and by straight start-ups such as Tinder and Bumble, which were founded a few years after Grindr. Collectively they have been changing the face of relationships. A study by Stanford University showed that online meeting was the most common way that couples got together in the USA – ahead of friends, family, college or church. The speed with which it happened is impressive – going from 2 per cent in 1990 to 40 per cent in 2017.[9] What we have learned from Grindr is that the ability to choose leads to ever more precision about who you want to date. Once you embark on a dynamic of segregation you can never go far enough – from dating to gay dating, to tribes, to tribes within tribes. There are now a plethora of dating apps that exclude people on the basis of their politics, religion, income or upbringing. Apps on the market now include much more specialized platforms such as Patrio (for patriotic conservative singles; their slogan

'Date Right'), Christian Mingle (a community of 15 million 'faith-driven singles'), GlutenfreeSingles and FarmersOnlyDating.[10]

It is still too early to predict reliably what the long-term consequences of this move online will be – but we can guess that it will lead to greater polarization. We know from offline behaviour that, when given the chance, people tend to seek out people just like them. 'Birds of a feather', we are told, 'flock together.' Of course what is meant by 'being similar' can change over time. In the USA race continues to be an important dividing line. In 2010 the census showed that 98 per cent of married white women had a white husband and 96 per cent of married black men had a black wife.[11] We have been told that 'assortative mating', the process whereby people with similar education levels and incomes pair up, already shoulders some of the blame for income inequality. Online dating may make the effect more pronounced: education levels are displayed prominently on dating profiles in a way they would never be offline.

Increasingly people are also seeking out partners who share their political views. A study by professors at Yale and Stanford Universities concluded that for Americans the politics of potential dates is as central as their education level, although it is still less important than race.[12] Opinion polls corroborate this trend. In 1960, 5 per cent of Republicans and Democrats reported that they would '[feel] "displeased" if their son or daughter married outside their political party'. By 2010, nearly 50 per cent of Republicans and over 30 per cent of Democrats felt 'somewhat' or 'very' unhappy at the prospect of interparty marriage.[13] And it's fair to say that society has become more polarized since then.

What is certainly true is that the move from mass society to microcommunities seen in the world of romance is also taking place in other aspects of life – spurred on by the logic of surveillance capitalism that is becoming increasingly scientific in identifying what people are interested in – and serving up more of it. The internet has allowed almost everyone on the planet to find a viable community of people who share whatever interests or obsessions make sense of their lives. As a result everyone can be part of an 'imagined majority' because they associate with others who share their interests.[14] What is new about the digital age is the ease and precision with which segregation and self-segregation can occur. So what are the societal consequences of allowing people to sort themselves into like-minded groups so easily?

Entire forests have been felled to provide paper for articles that have been written about 'filter bubbles' since 2016. One of the favourite political lines in debates used to be 'You can have your own opinions, but not your own facts'. But – in the era of fake news and social media – the reality is that every single self-identifying group can now have its own facts. Lots has been written about how the growth of digital and social media has changed our news diet. Increasingly we choose news providers who serve up what we want to hear. Psychologists tell us we are hardwired to disregard facts that do not conform to our prior beliefs, and now we do not need to see them at all.

Another effect is on the tone of our culture. In *Civilization and Its Discontents*, Freud describes how a measure of repression is key to civilization – the fact that people self-censor and hold back their darkest thoughts. But once people feel they are in a like-minded online community, they often let it all out.[15] Grindr was recently in the news for allowing its users to include derogatory declarations in their profiles such as 'no Asians', 'no blacks', 'no fatties', 'no femmes', 'no trannies' and 'masc4masc' (masculine for masculine).[16] Glossy magazines like *GQ* now run special features on 'the WhatsApp Trap' – showing how social media groups have given rise to 'micro-cultures' where men behave in ways they would never think acceptable in public, giving vent to racist, misogynistic and even criminal speech.[17] The accounts in the *GQ* piece include the rape fantasies of students in a Facebook group called 'Fuck Women. Disrespect Them All'; the abusive sex games of rugby players on WhatsApp, and the 'Exeter Five' law students who gloried in Enoch

Powell's 'Rivers of Blood' speech in a WhatsApp group called 'Dodgy Blokes Soc'. These and countless other examples show how the intimacy and segregation of digital platforms is leading to a veritable 'return of the repressed' – a regression to modes of behaviour which society had made unacceptable (as well as illegal).

The way the internet helps people segregate themselves changes the nature of political mobilization in ways we will explore more deeply in the next chapter. In the nineteenth and twentieth centuries people would come together in broad classes and communities that would often push for progress for large groups of society: a national health service, state education for all, a social safety net or universal pensions. But the multiple identities of the digital age tend to lead to ever more fragmentation. Movements that represent sectional identities like #MeToo and #BlackLivesMatter can be formed very quickly and have been inspiring in their advocacy of social justice. But what of groups that are motivated by universal values rather than addressing injustices towards particular groups? Sociologists fear that in our atomized age this is much harder – not least because of the way that the digital revolution is breaking down the very idea of a person into its component parts. It is challenging for traditional representative democracy to serve this politics with two parties rotating every four or five years.

Surveillance capitalism and the logic of globalization have reached deep into our lives and are breaking it up even more. Just as the supply chain of an iPhone includes parts made by 200 separate suppliers in forty-three countries across six continents, individuals are 'outsourcing' more and more of their private lives to experts who have a comparative advantage over us: from childcare and nutrition to dating coaches and personal trainers.[18] Increasingly, the state looks at us as taxpayers, car drivers, pedestrians, students, patients, or producers – rather than as whole people. And political parties will appeal to us as members of different identity groups rather than complex beings that are cross-pressured between different roles and desires.[19] Breaking people down into a collection of traits or skills deprives them of their humanity. As the sociologist Zygmunt Bauman argues, 'An assembly of traits can hardly be a moral object whose treatment is subjected to moral judgement . . . the very concept of information itself reduces the humanity of the categorised, whether the end in view is dating or killing.'[20] This is not an entirely new phenomenon. The slave market saw humans as commodities, while many societies still treat women as bearers of fertility, dowries, beauty, or family relations rather than autonomous agents. However, our technological advances have speeded up and intensified this compartmentalization. And once we are compartmentalized we are even more susceptible to the second dark feature of Connected Man: envy.

EMPATHY AND ENVY

The average user of Grindr spends ninety minutes a day scrolling through profiles, sorting people into different groups and sending them messages. By reducing humanity to a few data points – photos, size, education, tribe – it finally feels possible to compare the incomparable. Stripped back to our essence – or at least the version of our naked self that we want to present to the world – you can see the essential unity of mankind. This must be one of the reasons why being digitally connected has stretched people's empathetic horizons – allowing us to engage emotionally with people far away or that we have never met. Omar's tale is an inspiring story of a global community organizing itself to help people subjected to oppression. The examples of global outpourings of support and love are legion. In France, for instance, we might point to the Facebook profile *tricolores* after the 2015 Bataclan attack, and the huge fundraising campaign after Notre-Dame burned down in 2019.

Most people in the 1800s would not have known about a massacre or fire in a faraway place but our empathy today can be truly global.

However, in addition to increased empathy, connectivity has also created an epidemic of envy. Researchers have done a lot to expose the impact of social networks on body image[21] – laying out how unrealistic images of masculinity and femininity have led to a surge of eating disorders – and we are increasingly learning that the political impact of our age of comparison can be at least as great as its effect on mental health. In the last chapter we met René Girard's theory that many of our desires do not come from inside ourselves but rather are copied from others. We saw how the 'prophet of envy' inspired Peter Thiel to invest in Facebook – turning a $500,000 initial investment into a stake worth over a billion dollars.

Girard's theories were developed by studying great literature, but they have parallels in the sociological work of his contemporaries. In 1954, the sociologist Leon Festinger first proposed 'social comparison theory'.[22] He argued that most people define their identity by comparing themselves to others – drawing self-esteem when they think they are superior to their peers and losing it when the opposite occurs.

The researcher who did the most to explain how these socially con-structed identities can lead to conflict was a man called Henri Tajfel. For him the question was personal, as his whole life course was decided by a single decision he made about how to explain his own identity. Tajfel, who was born in Poland in 1919 to Jewish parents, went to Paris to study at the Sorbonne. He joined the French army to fight against the Nazis but ended up being taken as a prisoner of war by the Germans. When they questioned him he made the fateful decision of pretending to be French rather than Polish, which allowed him to be taken to a prisoner of war camp rather than a death camp. When he returned home he found most of his family and friends had been wiped out. Tajfel moved to Britain and devoted much of the rest of his life to understanding how his fate had come about.

Building on work by Festinger and others, Tajfel tried to find out how easily people would form social identities. In his early experiments he separated volunteers into two groups depending on what paintings they liked.[23] One group was given paintings by Kandinsky and the other by Paul Klee, and he told them to think of themselves as the 'in-group' and the 'out-group'. The two groups never met but they rapidly started thinking about themselves as a superior unit and to attribute negative qualities to the other group. When asked to distribute small sums of money, not only did the volunteers ensure their own group got more (even though this had no positive implication for them individually), they attempted to make the difference in income between the groups as big as possible, even if that meant receiving less themselves in absolute terms. What was most surprising is the fact that the competition between the new group identities became so important to participants that they were willing to suffer themselves if it meant that they could harm the other group.

Out of a series of similar experiments, Tajfel developed 'social identity theory', which revolutionized the way that people thought about conflict between groups. Before Tajfel's work, most people had seen inter-group conflict as an instrumental fight about competing interests. But Tajfel showed there is something more primordial at play. Membership of groups is a core part of our identity and source of pride, even if that membership is totally arbitrary. In order to feel better about ourselves we tend to ascribe positive attributes to our in-group's identity and to discriminate against people who are not part of it (the 'out-group'). Tajfel showed how stereotyping is a key part of defining people's identities, and splitting the world into 'us' and 'them'.

We know from these post-war experiments that identity comes as much from comparison as from internal features of individuals – and that once identities are formed they often result in conflict. But the big difference between now and the pre-digital age comes from *who* we compare our-selves to. In this new 'age of comparison', our frame of reference is suddenly global. By enabling us to benchmark ourselves in real time against the semi-fictional identities of the most successful people in the world, search engines like Google and social networks like Instagram promote intercon-tinental resentment. From Justin Bieber's flashy car collection to Kim Kardashian's unnatural hourglass figure to the backyard pools of celebri-ties or Gwyneth Paltrow's domestic bliss, we think that we can see how the other half lives.[24] One of the most dramatic features of the internet is that it allows people to meticulously curate their identities, creating seemingly perfect lives against which real life – the one we have to live in – always seems to fall short.

Every few years a big survey of people's values and wellbeing is con-ducted in dozens of countries around the world. 'In 1980, the world values survey found that economic wealth was unrelated to the levels of happiness in societies,' claims the political scientist Ivan Krastev. 'Back then Nigerians were as happy as West Germans. Recent surveys show that Nigerians are as happy as their incomes would predict them to be.'[25] The difference is that they are no longer comparing themselves to fellow Nigerians – but to the richest people in the world. We will go deeper into the political implications in places such as the UK and USA in the next chapter, but before we do that it is worth exploring briefly how this phenomenon plays out in Poland.

Not that many people in Warsaw have heard of Leon Festinger (or even their own compatriot Henri Tajfel), but the country's politicians would do well to study him if they want to understand how their politics has evolved over the last decade. Looking at traditional metrics for political success, you would have thought that the 2015 Polish election result was a foregone conclusion. Gross domestic product (GDP) had expanded by 46 per cent in inflation-adjusted terms over the past ten years, and average household incomes had grown by 30 per cent.[26] That extraordinary rise was the steepest in the European Union. But come election day, the government was swept from power. There had been a series of minor scandals that tarnished the government's reputation and the former Prime Minister Donald Tusk had taken a job as president of the European Council in Brussels. But that was not the most plausible explanation for the government's fate. 'The problem is that young Poles are not comparing their prospects today with what they were a decade ago or even with their parents', says Aleksandr Smolar, the chair of the Stefan Batory think-tank; 'they are comparing themselves with their schoolfriends who went to Germany and the UK.'[27] This shows that in the digital age, our sense of deprivation is no longer linked to the people who immediately surround us. Sociologists claim we have moved to a permanent, and 'free-floating', sense of grievance that is no longer fixed to a specific 'comparative group'.[28] As a result our sense of dissatisfaction is no longer 'relative' but 'universal'. Because it is not linked to a specific situation, there is nowhere we can go to get away from it.

AUTOMATION AND THE LOSS OF CONTROL

On dating apps, as you swipe left and right on the different profiles you feel like the master of the universe, deciding the fate of others with a simple flick of the thumb. Everything is automatic: a succession of candidates are lined up to await your judgement. But most users know that the real power resides with the algorithm that decides which images flash up on your screen in the first place. If the computer has decided you are not particularly attractive, you will not be presented with prospective partners who have supermodel looks. In order to 'improve the customer experience' all these decisions taken on your behalf are hidden from your view. Most of the time you are willing to put up with this situation, but occasionally your powerlessness becomes clear and you rage against the machine.

This shows the third dark side of the digital revolution. The fact that things are organized automatically makes them effortless and superficially empowering. But the black box of these algorithms is also leading to a sense that the world is out of control – something which has a dramatic impact on people and through that on our politics at a national and global level. Algorithmically driven platforms are nudging us to cede our decision-making on a daily basis, not just in the dating world but also telling us what books to read, what products to buy and when to exercise. Governments and companies are increasingly using algorithms and big data to make decisions about every aspect of our lives, from our children's exams to our ability to get a loan, be interviewed for a job or get medical care.[29] In the past, advertisers would joke that half of their spending was a total waste of money – they just didn't know which half. However, Google's surveillance capitalism has turned the art of selling into a science. They have managed to discover the holy grail of delivering a particular message to a particular person at the moment when they are most likely to act on it.[30]

In the place of rational choices between options, consumers find themselves increasingly nudged to buy products aimed specifically at them; and increasingly also with personalized prices.[31] For example, the travel website Orbitz has been accused of charging Mac users more than PC users for the same products – to reflect the fact that, statistically, they are probably wealthier.[32] The car firm Uber is allegedly investigating the idea of charging people with low batteries more for a ride.[33] And the stationery chain Staples is allegedly charging people less if they live in an area close to competitors.[34] If this manipulation is generalized there will no longer be a market of consumer choices, but a one-way flow of individualized 'offers you can't refuse' from active suppliers to passive consumers.[35] It seems unlikely that we will follow this process through to the logical conclusion of 8 billion 'markets of one', but one can see how algorithms could limit the real economic choices open to consumers.

Of course the threats big data and artificial intelligence pose to our freedom go well beyond the market. In the brave new world of the 2020s, all human beings have a 'digital unconscious' – a cache of Google searches, text messages and email that allows companies to understand us in some ways better than we know ourselves.[36] Every purchase we make, every search we conduct, every email we send has now become a confession thanks to the digital trails we leave on the internet and the metadata collected on our mobile phones. Google often knows if a woman is pregnant before she realizes it herself – just because of her search history. Tech companies with economies as big as countries shape what information we see, which people we listen to and what actions we take in ways that are driven by the pursuit of profit rather than the intention to deepen civil society.[37]

Their secret weapon in analysing all this data is artificial intelligence – the technology that AlphaGo used to defeat Lee Sedol in the last chapter. And one of the people who best understands the glories and the challenges of it is a professor called Stuart Russell. Slightly balding, with sparkling eyes and an open face, Russell retains an English accent in spite of decades living in the United States. As the computer scientist who co-wrote the standard artificial intelligence textbook back in the 1990s – it has now sold over 5 million copies – his name is familiar to many technologists. But when he talks about his job now, he warns that his field of research might endanger the survival of the species. Along with Elon Musk, Stephen Hawking, Max Tegmark, Nick Bostrom and many others, he has warned of the dangers of creating a superhuman intelligence that might end up – inadvertently – destroying mankind. Russell is a genial and optimistic companion but he is increasingly worried about the dangers of technology and in 2019 crystallized all his fears into a fascinating book called *Human Compatible: AI and the Problem of Control*. As is the case for many of the leading lights in his field, his greatest fear is that artificial intelligence will deprive humans of agency and could even endanger our survival.

The problem, he explains, is that artificial intelligence systems are single-minded at achieving any objective we set them: winning a game of chess, reducing carbon emissions, or speaking like humans. When they identify a strategy to fulfil that objective, they will stick with it whatever the consequences. For example, if you ask a self-driving car to get from A to B it will go there even if it might mean killing pedestrians. Or if you ask it to reduce carbon emissions, it might find that the most efficient way is to get rid of humans. If you put in a poorly defined objective, the system could take actions that humans hate, a situation that Russell describes as the 'King Midas problem'. 'King Midas specified his objective,' he said in an interview with *Vox* magazine, 'I want everything I touch turned to gold.' He got exactly what he asked for. Unfortunately, that included his food and his drink and his family members, and he died in misery and starvation. 'The genie grants you three wishes,' Russell explained. 'Always the third wish is "please undo the first two wishes because I ruined the world".'[38]

The most extreme fear that Russell and other AI-sceptics raise is of killer robots displacing humans to take over the world. But even if these nightmare scenarios do not take place, there are many ways that AI is destroying human agency. Artificial intelligence is only in its infancy but it has already led to thousands of Midas-like problems which make people feel angry or resentful. A lot has been written about the ways that algorithms inherit and accentuate biases and prejudices, so that outcomes can be markedly racist or sexist. One of the classic examples is the AI bot that the US digital giant Amazon built to help it with its hiring process. The company was forced to scrap it after a few years when it discovered that it had a major flaw: it didn't like women.

'Everyone wanted this holy grail,' one of the people involved in using the app at Amazon said. 'They literally wanted it to be an engine where I'm going to give you 100 resumés, it will spit out the top five, and we'll hire those.' But by 2015, the company realized that its system was systematically excluding female candidates. The problem was that it had been trained by giving it access to ten years of recruitment data within the company. In the male-dominated world of computer programming, most of the strong applications had come from men so the algorithm had taught itself to exclude women from its selections. Amazon is far from alone in being affected by biases in large data sets.[39]

It is perhaps unsurprising that one of the people who became most disturbed about the way that algorithms are taking over from human agency is also one of those who was most obsessed with power: Henry Kissinger. In his mid-nineties, Kissinger did not have his epiphany about the threat of artificial intelligence when scrolling through Tinder or Grindr but rather at a conference where experts on AI described the process of building the AlphaGo computer. He was fascinated to discover that unlike the Deep Blue chess computer that beat the World Chess Champion Garry Kasparov, the AlphaGo computer was not programmed by humans. It was self-trained – honing its gameplay by playing innumerable games against itself until it was able to beat the greatest Go player in the world. And even more important than winning, this computer developed new strategies and tactics that human players would never have tried. It seemed to have used a new kind of intelligence beyond our ken.

Kissinger was horrified. He asked himself what these self-learning machines would do with the knowledge, whether they would communicate with each other and how they would make choices. 'Was it possible,' he mused, 'that human history might go the way of the Incas, faced with a Spanish culture incomprehensible and even awe-inspiring to them?'[40] Kissinger may not understand much about AI (as some scientists observed when he published his critique), but he senses at a visceral level that his world – based on the centrality of the individual and the enlightenment project – is over. He worries that intelligence and moral consciousness are being separated. How will this new intelligence be used? How can computers which develop new ways of doing things reflect on the consequences of their actions?

The old idea was that liberalism was the most efficient way to run a country because people knew themselves better than the state did. The reason that central planning was abandoned by most countries wasn't that they objected to it on ideological grounds – it simply didn't work because a small group of people wasn't able to anticipate the needs of a very large group. But with big data, the government and corporations have much better insight into individuals than they used to. Kissinger had the right instinct that decision-making power – and even the very idea of sovereignty – is changing. In the pre-modern age, God was seen as the ultimate source of authority. With secularism, it was the state. With liberalism, it was the individual. But in the future, the algorithm will be sovereign. Computers powered by artificial intelligence may soon interpret a plethora of data points to make radical decisions about all aspects of our lives – in some areas this is already true. But these self-teaching machines are interested in finding what works rather than why it works. They use pattern recognition and big data to act efficiently – but are totally incapable of explaining to humans why these actions are optimal.[41]

Scientists like Russell and statesmen like Kissinger worry that the role of humans will be relegated to deciphering the significance of what AI systems are doing and to developing interpretations. In place of the Enlightenment and the centrality of human reason we will return to the classical oracle at Delphi which 'left to human beings the interpretation of its cryptic messages about human destiny'.[42] There are more fundamental reasons why data-driven algorithms lead to resentment and anger. First, they treat people as a set of disaggregated data points rather than moral actors and tend to classify them according to patterns. For example, when an algorithm was used to predict exam results in the UK, what mattered to the machine was avoiding grade inflation for the whole country rather than being fair to every individual within it. Second, algorithms by necessity act as if the future will be like the past. They look for patterns in historical data to make predictions about the future. However, this kind of data determinism makes it hard to allow for the possibility that individuals can change, one of the core ideas of human freedom.[43] But above all decisions made within traditional institutions have accountability built into them, whereas many of these decisions are being made without scrutiny, in the 'black box' of an algorithm, with no right of appeal.

As we have seen from the above, almost all of the most positive features of connectivity also have a dark side, a digital double that drives people apart. The quest to connect particular communities also leads to segregation into different identity groups. The same network effects that spread empathy have also led to an epidemic of envy. And attempts to empower people through artificial intelligence have deprived them of agency. All these tendencies make connected people susceptible to conflict – and also explain why, when they congregate together in national politics, they are likely to support belligerent policies. That is what we explore in the next chapter.

CHAPTER THREE:

NATIONAL CULTURES OF UNPEACE: THE POLITICS OF TAKING BACK CONTROL

They called it the Occupation of Prague. On 21 August 2016, a jeep flying an ISIS flag drove into the Old Town Square, filled with bearded men shooting guns, crying 'Allahu Akbar'. Their leader shouted out 'We are bringing you the light of true faith' as he fired a submachine gun into the air. Panicked onlookers ran off, knocking over tables and chairs, leaving the injured behind in their wake. It took some time for anyone to realize that the imam leading the charge, Martin Konvicka, was an anti-immigration activist rather than an ISIS terrorist. Equipped with a camel, a goat, detachable beards and fake guns, Konvicka and his supporters had planned the event to show what life would be like if too many Muslim refugees were allowed to come into the Czech Republic.[1] The police broke up the performance before it reached its climax – a mock beheading of an infidel – but Konvicka took to Facebook to declare the exercise a success.[2] The date they had chosen was deliberately symbolic: the anniversary of the Soviet-led invasion of 1968.[3]

Although his tactics are eccentric to say the least, Konvicka's protest was perfectly designed to tap into the new mood of our connected politics. It was calibrated to exploit each of the vulnerabilities we explored in the last chapter: polarization around identity, envy and a sense among native communities that their countries are being changed by forces over which they have little control. The new nationalism it represents is a product of connectivity. It is part of the reason why geopolitics is tending towards competition rather than cooperation.

It is ironic that only a few weeks before Konvicka's demonstration there was a more conventional protest on some of the same themes in London – only this one was directed against immigration from Eastern European countries such as the Czech Republic. Standing on the vast stage of Wembley Stadium for the final debate in the referendum campaign on British membership of the EU, the politician Boris Johnson called upon his fellow citizens to take back control of their borders, their finances and their lives. 'If we vote to leave,' he roared, 'this Thursday could be our country's Independence Day.'

Konvicka and Johnson may not look like natural heirs to Thomas Jefferson, Mahatma Gandhi and Jomo Kenyatta, but the themes of subjugation and exclusion that they channel are immediately recognizable to anti-colonial movements from earlier eras. 'The colonized world is a world divided in two . . . inhabited by different species,' Frantz Fanon claimed in his book *The Wretched of the Earth*, which became a bible of decolonization in the 1960s. He talked about a compartmentalized world where the majority native population lived in different areas, cultures and economic conditions from the elites. He also talked about the emotional toll on natives who felt disrespected, marginalized and accused of prejudice and unreason.

The chimes of freedom have rung down through the decades, galvanizing movements of national liberation, conjuring up new nations who claimed their own states and leading to an ever more fragmented map of the world.[4] And, on 21 June 2016, Alexander Boris de Pfeffel Johnson made a bid to launch a fifth wave of decolonization. Only this one would be different: a process of internal decolonization. It was an attempt by the 'indigenous' majority to free themselves from the perceived control of cosmopolitan elites and the immigrant populations they had imported. And this quest for secession was rapidly mirrored in the pro-Remain regions who were equally keen to free themselves from the new independence-seeking elites that Brexit has produced. The Scottish National Party has put the question of Scottish independence back on the cards while a petition for an independent London attracted an improbable 175,000 signatures in the days after the Brexit referendum. One of the paradoxes of the connected world is that almost everyone can make common cause with enough like-minded people to be part of a viable political community. The more connected the world becomes, the more fragmented. And connectivity gives each of these constituencies reasons to envy, fear and conflict with one another. In that sense it leads to growing conflict *within* nations.

MOBILIZED MINORITIES AND THREATENED MAJORITIES

In the industrial era, politics amounted to a struggle between well-defined classes over the distribution of wealth. The mass labour movement was born out of the factories while parties on the right were spawned by the churches that united the petite bourgeoisie and the capitalist classes. As the national mass media rose they became the main battleground for these catch-all parties to play out their contest for power. The leading sociologist Manuel Castells has argued that the internet creates a different kind of politics by allowing new groups to crystallize around identity and values.[5] It has helped to spawn the new wave of 'decolonization' by allowing both minorities and majorities to cluster in novel ways.

Back in 2002 a book called *The Emerging Democratic Majority* by John B. Judis and Ruy Teixeira electrified Democratic Party strategists in America with a vision of mobilizing, growing Asian, Hispanic and African-American minority populations that were gradually outnumbering a shrinking white population in the USA.[6] It was by following their playbook that Barack Obama and Joe Biden managed to win majorities. But just as significant was the counter-mobilization of white people who felt provoked by this new landscape, allowing Donald Trump to win the presidency in 2016. This was a powerful instance of a new political phenomenon: the mobilization of 'threatened majorities', majorities that behave like minorities. The far-right French intellectual Renaud Camus described the phenomenon in an influential book, *Le Grand Remplacement*, where he warns that within one to two generations France's European population will be replaced by visible minorities – as a result of immigration and differential birth-rates. His right-wing message has echoed across the world – from Poland to the USA – where citizens complain they are becoming 'strangers' in their own countries. When President Trump promised, in his victory speech on 9 November 2016, that 'the forgotten men and women of our country will be forgotten no longer', he was also making himself the voice of the new 'wretched of the earth', the white population that feels it has been colonized in reverse.[7] European empires may have conquered and exploited much of the Global South, dehumanizing and disenfranchising millions around the world, but now globalization is making former colonial centres feel they themselves are being disenfranchised.

In this world of connected identity politics the goal is no longer to persuade people to change their minds but rather to identify people who agree with you already and to frame the debate in a way that ensures you have a majority. With micro-targeting and big data, political parties are able to tailor their messages and messengers to the individual rather than relying on mass campaigns. But the Cambridge Analytica scandal revealed an extra level of ambition: appealing to people's psychology as much as their views. Their goal was to hack people's brains – getting behind their conscious minds to manipulate their actions. Although Cambridge Analytica's staff later admitted that their claims when pitching for business massively outstripped their actual abilities, their ambitions point to the way that politics has evolved in lockstep with developing technology.

The risk is that, through 'fake news', social media, big data and 'gaslighting', political parties give up trying to persuade us and resort instead to manipulating us. Deepfake technology is making it easier to manipulate video, and AI is rapidly improving its ability to write cogent arguments without human assistance. As technology researchers experiment with computers that are plugged directly into our brains – such as Elon Musk's Neuralink – it raises troubling questions about whether programmers might manipulate our emotions without even going through the conscious parts of our brains.[8]

HUMILIATION AND POWERLESSNESS

Some have argued that the new decolonization movement is a response to the economic inequality inherent in globalization. They talk about how the knowledge economy, the rise of robots, the collapse of manufacturing and a surge in trade and migration – coupled with austerity and shrinking safety nets – has left many worse off. An alternative explanation sees a cultural backlash against cosmopolitanism and cultural change.[9] In our connected world many of the economic complaints are at core indivisible from culture. David Abernethy's magisterial history of the colonial experience shows how European empires reshaped the economies, political institutions and even values of the countries they occupied by moving capital, technology and people across borders. 'A legacy of colonial rule,' he explains, 'is a high level of vulnerability to externally generated economic and technological changes.'[10] In other words, colonized countries would see their economies turned on their heads because of decisions taken in faraway places. One of the most powerful indicators of the capriciousness of these changes are the names that European settlers gave to many colonies. They often had little to do with local customs and more to do with the commodities that Europeans wanted to grow or extract: Cape Cod, Minas Gerais, Argentina, Rio de Oro, Gold Coast, Côte d'Ivoire.[11] Populists are arguing that these dynamics are now being reversed and that it is now the indigenous populations of the West on the receiving end of economic forces they cannot control.

The fact that Boris Johnson made his claim to lead an 'independence movement' in the heart of London was particularly resonant. This is the city that spawned the largest empire (according to one historian only twenty-two countries have not been invaded by Britain[12]) and in the process built a world of connectivity. The historian Eric Hobsbawm has written compellingly about how the combination of the Industrial Revolution and the empire led to the entire world economy being built on, or rather around, Britain.[13] That British empire is long gone but London remains the most connected city in the world, with the highest broadband use,[14] the most international flights[15] and the world's largest foreign exchange market.[16] The EU referendum showed that in today's Britain, the majority do not regard themselves as heirs to the colonial masters of the global economy; rather they see themselves as a 'colonized people', at the mercy of a cosmopolitan London elite. As Fanon says of the colonial world, 'The ruling species is first and foremost the outsider from elsewhere, different from the indigenous population.'

In Britain's European debate this critique was predominantly about migration, which was used to show the difference in perspective between the new elites and the citizens of the displaced majority. For business leaders and professional classes, migration is seen as an unqualified bonus – providing better-qualified, harder-working and cheaper staff and adding to the cultural richness of these islands. But although the British economy as a whole benefited, many citizens felt that the gains were not shared with them. Individual neighbourhoods in areas that attract large migratory flows have not been given additional resources to provide housing, school places or doctors. And wages in some regions and sectors – such as construction – had downward pressure.

Other countries have similar tales of dual economies and societies. Donald Trump used trade with China and immigration from Mexico to symbolize the divisions between coastal elites and the majority white population. We saw in the first chapter how resonant the Chinese issue has been as a mobilizer.

A bestselling essay by the geographer Christophe Guilluy, *La France Périphérique*, describes two competing Frances. On the one hand, the country of the metropoles which are gleaming examples of happy globalization filled with the managerial classes and hard-working immigrants. On the other, the majority of the country – 60 per cent of the population – who live in small and medium-sized towns and villages that draw no benefits from globalization.

Within the eurozone, when countries such as Greece and Spain suffered a banking and sovereign debt crisis, their governments found themselves listening to diktats from international lenders rather than responding to the desires of the citizens who voted for them.[17] And because of the role of Berlin in designing the bailouts, the leaders of left-wing parties in Europe's debtor nations complained about being reduced to the status of a 'German colony'.

Eastern European countries such as Hungary and Poland may not be in the euro but they feel they are being turned into peripheral countries by German supply chains. In 2017 Polish Prime Minister Mateusz Morawiecki referred to international investors as 'colonizers' and argued that Poland had been reduced to a German economic colony by joining value chains which trap it in a low-skills economy while the profits are repatriated to the corporate headquarters.[18]

The quest for control for all those 'independence movements' is about money, but it is just as much about wounded pride. Living in a world of hyper-comparison, frustrated citizens feel they are losing control of their futures while seeing others across borders surging ahead.

Advocates of connectivity have changed the way they measure progress so that it reflects their aspirations for a connected world – and makes the effects on the losers of that world almost invisible. Internationalists have often tried to gather data that treats the planet and nations as a whole. This has led to figures on global GDP growth or global carbon emissions. By looking at aggregate data it is possible to say that globalization has been good for the world and good for every country within it.[19] But the aggregate data hides the unequal way those benefits have been distributed.

In the USA, the top 1 per cent earned 12 per cent of market income in 1979 and almost 20 per cent in 2016. For the bottom half of the population, these figures were 20 per cent in 1979 and 13 per cent in 2016.[20] It's true to say that, on average, everyone got richer – but it is equally true to say that the poor got poorer. The same distortions emerge from looking at climate change, where the negative impacts like pollution are unequally spread.

There is a parallel between the development of economics for a connected world and attempts in earlier ages to develop a common language. The founders of Esperanto tried to integrate the features of the most popular languages in the world to develop a common lingua franca. But although their motives were unimpeachable, the result of their efforts was to develop a deracinated language that was less expressive than its constituent parts. The creation of 'Esperanto economics' has similarly meant that much of our data on global progress is divorced from the lived experience of ordinary citizens. It prevents the winners from understanding the plight of the losers while increasing the latter's resentment. It is bad enough to see your standard of living stagnate without being told that it makes you a winner.

CULTURES OF PEACE VS. CULTURES OF UNPEACE

Boris Johnson's Brexit campaign positioned itself as an independence movement, but Brexit was an act of aggression as well as secession. One pollster told me about focus groups she conducted with Leave voters. 'Don't you believe the economic warnings from the Bank of England and the IMF?' she asked one voter in the north of England. 'Of course I do,' came the answer, 'but that is their economy not mine, and it's about time that people in London learned what it is like to deal with economic pain.' The goal for some was literally to weaponize connectivity – or rather to weaponize the removal of connectivity – to punish other groups in society.

It reflects the way the rules of politics are changing – from a peace-time mindset to one characterized by unpeace. I found out about it when my think-tank commissioned an opinion poll of 60,000 voters across Europe.[21] Despite the fact that the European Union is the world's most successful peacebuilding project, our poll revealed that, across the EU, almost three in ten voters (28 per cent) believed that war between EU member states is a realistic possibility. Even more surprising was the fact that among young people a majority in almost all member states agreed with this statement.

The European project is founded on consensus, reason, logic, and the rationale of win-win cooperation. Agreed-upon facts and common knowledge are central to this rational decision-making. In this world, data is in itself a peacebuilding exercise – its purpose is to show that there is a common truth.[22] But our survey shows that in present-day Europe, this common understanding has eroded.

In our poll around half the European voting population – 187 million – lives still in the European peace project. They think that war between EU countries is impossible. These 'peaceniks' believe in the power of facts and cooperation, and they are voting for pro-European parties. The other half lives in a Europe with warrior values. In their world facts and knowledge matter less than emotions, energy, mobilization and commitment.[23] Speed of initiative and rapid responses take priority over the careful, time-consuming evaluation of alternatives and cautiously constructed responses. This is not 'war' in the old-fashioned sense of two armies facing each other but a long-term, continuous conflict where the line between aggressors and civilians is blurred and the battle is for 'hearts and minds' more than territory.

These changes to the form, content and cadence of politics in all developed nations are already transforming international relations. A politics centred around independence, anger and control has started to lead to closing borders, rolling back free trade and reclaiming power from international institutions. Rather than free trade and cooperation to solve global problems such as pandemics and climate change, there has been a struggle by individual countries to get ahead and extract as many benefits as they can from a shrinking global pie. Rather than progressing towards one world, it opens the way for competition and a perpetual age of unpeace.

CHAPTER FOUR:

THE GEOPOLITICS OF CONNECTIVITY: WHY COUNTRIES COMPETE RATHER THAN WORK TOGETHER

Four decades have passed since Iranian students crying 'Death to America!' seized the US embassy in Tehran. They held dozens of Americans captive for 444 days in a hostage crisis that was one of the most humiliating setbacks for American foreign policy since the founding of the republic. Although the hostages were released in early 1981 after the two countries struck a deal, the embassy did not reopen.

Today, the old embassy complex serves as a training centre for Iran's Revolutionary Guards. Next to memorials for Ayatollah Khomeini and the 'Martyrs of the Revolution', there is a 'Den of Espionage' museum dedicated to preserving the memory of American perfidy. On a warm afternoon in 2014, I was shown around the museum by a young Revolutionary Guard, who told me about the evils of American culture while simultaneously advising me in forensic detail of all the errors in *Argo*, the Hollywood movie set during the embassy siege. They have preserved all the relics of America's imperial behaviour: painfully reconstituting the shredded top secret papers, exhibiting bugs and tape recorders, mainframe computers the size of rooms, as well as the remains of the American helicopter which crashed in a botched rescue attempt during the hostage crisis. The grand staircase leading visitors into the embassy has been transformed by graffiti artists into a graphic reconstruction of American foreign policy including the downing of Iran Air flight 655 in 1988, the attack on the World Trade Center in 2001, the invasions of Afghanistan and Iraq, and the military prisons in Guantanamo Bay and Abu Ghraib.

The whole complex is like a time capsule: an anachronistic vision of the future packed with now obsolete technologies. It is preserved as an open wound that can regularly be salted when Iran is in need of an external enemy to rally the population. But today's Iranians are less concerned with these old-fashioned expressions of American dominance than with the high-tech pressure they have had to endure more recently. The fact that it is impossible to buy an entrance ticket to the museum by debit or credit card – or indeed to buy anything anywhere in Iran with a debit or credit card – is because of the surgical way that Washington has used its control of the dollar to exclude a country of 83 million people from global financial markets (much more on that in the next chapter). And young revolutionaries such as my guide bristle at the fact that Iran was the target of the first act of cyberwar at the hands of the Americans and Israelis, a blow that continues to haunt the country until this day.

As noted earlier, Carl von Clausewitz famously described war as the continuation of politics by 'other means'. But the 'other means' used in today's Middle East is connectivity itself. Iran is a country whose young people have embraced the digital revolution and whose population is connected to distant corners of the world through links of kith and kin, a shared Shia religious identity and a history of trading that goes back two millennia to the time of the silk roads. And today, maybe as much as any other country, Iran finds itself at the heart of the new age of unpeace, both victim and perpetrator of the connectivity conflicts tearing our world apart. Its situation tells us a lot about how connectivity is creating conflict at a global level. It shows how the ties of globalization and the digital revolution have given both Tehran and its enemies a reason, as well as an opportunity, to embrace conflict. From Iran's plight we can see how connectivity has made conflict less expensive, helped to manufacture and stoke grievances, and led to a balance of power that makes the embrace of conflict attractive to the weak and strong alike.

INTERDEPENDENCE AND CONFLICT

Statesmen and scholars have argued for decades over whether interdependence can stop war – or if it actually creates it.[1] And people in the Middle East have provided a living petri dish for this experiment.

Liberals, starting with Immanuel Kant in his brilliant eighteenth-century essay *Perpetual Peace*, have claimed that economic interdependence promotes peace. Open markets remove one of the most important historical causes of war: the need to get access to raw materials and consumers for products. If any state can get access to anything through trade, why would it spill blood? What's more, the very process of trading creates deep bonds between the elites of different countries and makes them feel less alien. Once these bonds are in place there are powerful interests on both sides of the border who can lobby their governments not to resort to war. The so-called 'Dell Theory of Peace' stipulates that war is impossible between any countries connected by supply chains such as those of the Dell computer company, as it would be prohibitively expensive and disruptive.[2] Liberals also believe in the power of international institutions, which can develop a life of their own and become advocates of common interests. It is this kind of thinking which led the British, French and German governments – after the chaos of the Iraq War – to suggest a diplomatic route out of the Iranian nuclear crisis. Back in 2005, rather than going to war with Tehran they sought to integrate it into the global economy and take away its reasons for wanting nuclear weapons. They hoped to replace the regional arms race with a logic of de-escalation.

On the other hand, so-called 'realists' claim that links between countries can create insecurity which makes conflict more likely. The political economist Albert Hirschman pointed out decades ago that trading relations rarely benefit both sides equally, and that this asymmetry can lead to tensions. Sometimes the country on the wrong side of the bargain can be worried that trading links are changing the balance of power between them.[3] Sometimes, the relationship can be so skewed in favour of one side that the other can afford to forgo trade at relatively little cost. And some leaders have used military expansion to liberate themselves from economic dependence on others, using the arms trade to stimulate domestic demand.[4] What's more, decisions about war and peace are rarely made by economic ministries or influenced by companies, so even if these groups are against war their voices may not be heard.[5] That is certainly true in Iran, where different branches of power operate according to different logics. The diplomats who spend their time negotiating nuclear deals with Europeans do not control the Revolutionary Guards who are running paramilitary campaigns across the region. And it is precisely the fear of entanglement with Western economies – who might later blackmail Iran – which has led the hard-liners in the Iranian system to throw a spanner in the works of the nuclear negotiations at every turn.

Recent empirical work casts these debates about the theory of war, peace and connectivity in a new light – proving that both sides are right. Interdependence does seem to make *conventional war* less likely, as the liberals have claimed. But the bad news is that it also makes *conflict* between nations more likely, as the realists have long feared. The

American political scientist Eric Gartzke came to this conclusion after studying over 100,000 political, economic and military conflicts involving 150 countries over several decades.[6]

Gartzke compares conflict between nations to a game of chicken – like James Dean and Corey Allen in *Rebel Without a Cause*. Both sides know that if they collide it will be catastrophic – but there are benefits to be reaped if your opponent concedes first. And so they look for ways of proving they will not give way in order to increase their credibility and make it more likely that the other will blink. In a nuclear age there is huge danger in military confrontation, and even conventional war now demands sacrifices which few populations are comfortable making. Because war is so costly, no state is likely to launch one over a minor disappointment. The danger, therefore, is that minor frustrations build up until they are collectively important enough to provoke a war. This is where interdependence comes in. If states have multiple economic and human ties with each other, they have an opportunity to signal their unhappiness without paying the heavy price of all-out war. Manipulating interdependence, says Gartzke, creates a 'middle way' between talk and war, reducing militarized conflict but increasing non-militarized conflict over a greater variety of minor issues. It is the very fact that war is so costly that makes countries look for cheaper ways to conflict with each other, and the greater the links between nations, the more opportunity there is to engage in conflict.

So, if Gartzke's data are right, the natural partner of Kant's 'perpetual peace' is perpetual conflict. When I ask him if this is true, he agrees. Gartzke compares growing interdependence to family dinners like Thanksgiving – bringing people into close proximity for periods of time can promote love but it often also brings out tensions. Binding countries together doesn't just create harmony, it multiplies the opportunities and reasons for conflict. I don't think there are many people in the Middle East who celebrate Thanksgiving but it is a region with a growing population that finds itself more and more closely bound together. These linkages have resulted in tensions that occasionally erupt in heartbreaking wars. But although the wars get most of the headlines, the biggest rivalries are born out in Gartzke's grey zone between war and peace.

LOW-COST CONFLICT

In the 1980s, there were daily reports of Iran's bloody war with neighbouring Iraq. Images of that conflict echoed those of the First World War: trench warfare, barbed wire, bayonet charges, manned machinegun posts and poison gas attacks. The body count – 500,000 Iraqi and Iranian soldiers dead – also belonged to that era. It was a rare conflict that united the Cold War antagonists – the USA and the USSR – which both ended up arming the Iraqi tyrant Saddam Hussein to undermine Iran's revolutionary regime. Seared by that devastating war, Iran vowed to avoid further mass conflicts, although it was a major, if accidental, beneficiary of American interventions which took out their implacable enemy Saddam Hussein and the hostile Taliban regime in neighbouring Afghanistan.

With the end of the Cold War it was once again possible to get involved in military confrontations without risking nuclear Armageddon. As the Soviet empire unravelled there were a host of conflicts that broke out in Yugoslavia and in the post-Soviet space over the borders and make-up of new states. Western countries increasingly found themselves engaged in 'small wars' to prevent genocide, to stop the flow of weapons of mass destruction or go after terrorists. Back in 2003 when Americans and Europeans were debating whether to topple Saddam Hussein, the big joke among pugnacious neo-conservatives was to say: invading Iraq is for wimps, real men go to Iran. But over time it became clear that the cost of the trillion-dollar wars in Afghanistan and Iraq was anything but small. And so states started to look for cheaper ways of exercising power over Iran.

In Washington and Western capitals governments began to look for interventions that did not involve ground troops. Meanwhile Russia led the way in pioneering interventions below the threshold of formal war, inspiring China and many Middle Eastern countries with their model. Think-tanks like RAND and the CSIS that once made their names studying nuclear weapons, preventive war and humanitarian intervention are now producing reports on 'hybrid warfare' which chart out the ways in which great powers compete for power in the grey zone between war and peace.[7] They list tactics such as interference in elections, disinformation and fake news, cyber attacks, drone attacks and financial influence.

Iran was the target of the first act of cyberwar – one that continues to haunt it until this day. It was making rapid progress with its nuclear programme and within grasping distance of having a 'break-out capability' – gathering enough material and know-how that its progress towards nuclear weapons would be unstoppable. But then, in 2010, disaster struck its nuclear plant in Natanz. Almost a thousand centrifuges blew up over a three-month period, setting the programme back by many months. The psychological effect was even greater: spreading paranoia that a rogue scientist might be on site and more generally leading the Iranians to lose faith in their own capabilities. The cause was the 'Stuxnet' computer worm which exploited a weakness in the plant's Siemens operating system. Discovered in 2010, this cyber attack, which is alleged to have been conducted by Israel and the USA, slowed down the Iranian bomb programme by as much as two years – longer, in all likelihood, than would have resulted from an airstrike. At the time it was so novel that it was not yet understood as an act of military aggression. It existed in a nether region between war and peace, neither a normal act of exchange nor one aggressive enough to count as a declaration of war. It was emblematic of the grey zone that has characterized Middle Eastern geopolitics ever since.

Once Tehran discovered what had happened it was traumatized – and the authorities vowed to develop their own grey zone capabilities. Their starting point was to make it harder for others to infiltrate Iran's own systems. Like many countries across the Middle East, it took a leaf from the Chinese playbook and developed an impressive infrastructure of online censorship and surveillance – deploying filters to exclude messages from foreign powers as well as restricting the opportunities for Iranians to congregate.[8] It took less than two years after Stuxnet for Iran to launch a cyber attack of its own against American critical infrastructure.[9] While Iran mainly targets adversaries like Saudi Arabia and Israel, its missions against the US include Operation Ababil (a.k.a. Mahdi), which targeted the financial sector and a New York dam in 2012; an attack on the Sands Casino in Las Vegas that did $40 million in damage; and the ongoing probing of American electricity grids.[10]

Iranians like to joke that the outline of their country resembles a Persian cat, which may be one of the reasons that so many of the top Iranian hacking groups have adopted feline names. Collectives with names such as Helix Kitten and Rocket Kitten have been accused of targeting defence companies, financial services, energy groups, water and electricity grids in Saudi Arabia, Israel and the USA. One group, Charming Kitten, in 2017 hacked the entertainment company HBO and released unbroadcast episodes of *Game of Thrones* when the company refused to pay a ransom. Two years later it was accused by Microsoft of attempting to interfere in Donald Trump's campaign for the 2020 presidential election.[11]

But even more eye-catching than the exploits of Charming Kitten was the identity of one of its alleged operatives. Monica Elfriede Witt is not one of the children of the Iranian Islamic revolution although she was born in 1979, the year that the US embassy in Tehran was taken under siege. She comes from an unremarkable Christian family in El Paso, Texas, and didn't think much about the Middle East before she joined the air force in 1997. As part of her service she trained as a linguist, specializing in Farsi, and was given top secret security clearance and sent on covert intelligence missions. After the Iraq War she was decorated with an Air Medal by President George W. Bush and went on to receive a number of other medals for her distinguished service. She was in military service until 2008, serving in Saudi Arabia, Qatar and Iraq. But in 2008 she left the air force, studied for a master's degree, converted to Islam and began condemning a lot of the things she had seen in her military service, including what she described as 'drone strikes, extra-judicial killings and atrocities against children'. In 2013 she turned up at the Iranian embassy in Kabul, determined to tell all, and later in the year defected to Iran. From there she began working on behalf of Iran's Revolutionary Guard, targeting former colleagues. Using a fake Yahoo! email address and a Facebook account, she attempted to put malware on their computers that would capture their keystrokes, gain access to web cameras and monitor their activity. She was charged – in her absence – in a US court in 2019 on two counts of espionage.[12]

Her defection was one of the most visible symbols of the way that Tehran has gone from victim to perpetrator in the cyberwars. Since 2005, thirty-four countries are suspected of sponsoring cyber attacks; the Council on Foreign Relations claims that China, Russia, Iran, and North Korea have sponsored three-quarters of all suspected operations.[13] Iran's recent struggles show how much international relations have changed this century: Iran's twenty-first-century conflicts have an entirely different character from its war with Iraq, centred around connectivity and waged through the infrastructure of globalization.

THE GRIEVANCE FACTORY

The Den of Espionage museum is not the only focus of anti-American propaganda in Tehran. Opposition to America has been part of Iranian identity since the Islamic Revolution in 1979. But in my discussions with the young guard and other Iranians on several trips to Iran, I couldn't help feeling there is almost a rote quality to the rhetoric against the USA. The most bitter anger is now reserved for a less distant rival, Saudi Arabia. The gulf which divides Tehran from Riyadh is narrower than the ocean which separates it from the United States. Although they have broken off their diplomatic relationship and have limited trade they are not able to escape all the intense contact that comes from sharing a neighbourhood. The two countries are doomed to rub up against one another in innumerable ways, and this intimate coexistence has become a factory for grievances.

The geopolitics of the Middle East has been transformed by the developments we explored in the last two chapters. A new tribalism, a sense of victimhood and a desire for control are just as central here as they were to Brexit and the rise of Trump. In recent years identity politics has displaced more universal identities such as pan-Arabism and nationalism. And, of all the tribal identities that have resurfaced, the most important is the schism between Shia and Sunni. These sectarian religious identities, once suppressed by authoritarian leaders during the Cold War, have come back with a vengeance after the Arab Spring and are being exploited by the Iranian and Saudi regimes.

To see this for myself, I travelled 100 miles south of Tehran to Qom, the spiritual capital of global Shiism, which has become a haven not just for Persians but for Shiite Arabs from farther afield. The streets are packed with tens of thousands of students and clerics from around the world. Dressed in black robes with white turbans, these cosmopolitan worshippers bustle along the streets between the domes and minarets of religious buildings, combining study and prayer with the banalities of everyday living. A stone's throw from the beautiful shrine of Fatima Masumeh and its famous seminary is a street full of Arab shops, houses and conveniences. 'It's like a Chinatown,' a young Persian resident of Qom told me, 'only it's filled with Arabs.' The 'Arab street' – as it's known locally – is a haven for Shia escaping from persecution elsewhere in the Arab world. The city, with its scholarship, its region-wide charitable work and public communications, is the embodiment of Iran's leadership aspirations, the same ambitions that have led Tehran to defend Shia shrines in Najaf, Samarra, Karbala and Damascus.

As Iran reinvents itself as a champion of global Shia, Saudi Arabia is placing ever more emphasis on its vocation as protector-in-chief of the Sunni peoples. Whenever I travel to Riyadh – whether speaking to Saudi princes, cabinet ministers or technocrats in the oil ministry – I find Iran's obsession with Saudi Arabia more than reciprocated. They see the evil intentions of the mullahs behind every setback and live in perpetual fear of being outwitted by their Persian neighbours.

Because Tehran has not wanted to fight a conventional war against its rivals, it has used cyber attacks, cultural ties and proxy militias to increase its regional influence. In its struggle against Saudi Arabia, it has reached out to pro-Shia groups in its neighbourhood including in Iraq, Lebanon, Bahrain, Yemen and, most visibly, in Syria. It spent an estimated $15 billion propping up the pro-Iranian Bashar al-Assad and sent some 10,000 operatives to Syria between 2011 and 2014. This number omits non-Iranian forces backed by Tehran, which the *Wall Street Journal* put at 130,000 in 2014.[14] The biggest investments have been in movements like Hamas and Hezbollah. And, as it developed its cyber capabilities, it included an online dimension to its support for rebel movements. Iran has invested in a whole series of cyber proxies in all the countries where it is competing for influence, such as Cyber Hezbollah, Cyber Hamas, the

Syrian Electronic Army (SEA), and the Yemen Cyber Army. They have conducted cyber attacks on Iranian enemies like the Israeli Defence Force as well as engaging in disinformation campaigns.

Iran has also launched a series of highly visible attacks to disrupt its rival's connections. Many analysts believe Tehran was behind the Shamoon cyber attack on Saudi Aramco, the world's most valuable oil company, which destroyed around 30,000 computers and disrupted the company's ability to trade oil and gas in 2012. This was followed in 2019 by Iranian drone attacks on Aramco's oil facilities that affected half of Saudi Arabia's oil exports. Underpinning all of its campaigns to disrupt others in the cyber-realm is an impressive infrastructure to police its own population's access to the internet, powered by Chinese and Russian technology.

Saudi Arabia has reciprocated in kind – backing armed groups and militias to take the fight to Iran's proxies in Syria, Yemen, Bahrain and Lebanon, among other places. It has set up a series of troll factories to amplify its messages on social media (in 2019 Twitter suspended a stunning 90,000 fake accounts designed to spread Saudi propaganda).[15] It has also cemented its links with Iran's sworn enemies, the USA and Israel. After the chaos in Iraq and Afghanistan, the United States did not want to invade another Middle Eastern country, so it used 'all measures short of war' to slow the Iranian nuclear programme and persuade Iranian citizens to overthrow their religious leaders. The sanctions to which Iran was subject were of unprecedented ferocity. In the next chapter we will explore how they amputated Tehran from the global economy.

In some ways, the regional competition between Iran and Saudi Arabia echoes the global one between Washington and Beijing. They are each other's favourite rivals and their competition suffuses every aspect of national life. Just like Washington and Beijing, the more Iran and Saudi Arabia compete with one another, the more similar they become.

Both states are vying to be the face of modern Islamic rule in which religion and nationhood are equally important, in Saudi under the crown of the House of Saud, and in Iran under the Ayatollah's turban. Both want to become the economic powerhouse of the Middle East. They competed traditionally in oil markets; now they're in a race to diversify their economies. Both have developed alliances with militias to wage proxy conflicts against each other.

THE END OF ORDER

With the centenary of the First World War many people asked whether history would repeat itself. In 1914 globalization came apart because the great powers went to war with one another. As the liberal order frays and geopolitical competition returns, it is natural that people fear the same thing could happen again. But the world of 1914 was a far cry from our era of ambiguity, rapid change and disruption. The defining principle of that age – one that had been in place since the Peace of Westphalia – was the boundary between domestic and foreign policy. Great powers agreed not to interfere in each other's internal affairs.

But the reality is that the world of the 2020s could see exactly the opposite dynamics occur. The big danger today is that globalization may be destroyed precisely because the great powers do not want to go to war. In the absence of war they are manipulating the links between their countries and causing everyone to see interdependence as a vulnerability.

In our world of networks, challenges like terrorism, cyber warfare, climate change, and refugee flows have dissolved the distinction between internal and external, between domestic and foreign. And there is no longer a clear divide between war and peace.

In the physical realm, many are trying out new kinds of coercion that fall short of conventional warfare through special forces and 'little green men', coastguards impinging on international waters, or proxy wars through funding rebel groups. This is supplemented by a perpetual conflict online, from misinformation, hacking and leaking to the destruction of nuclear facilities.

Many had hoped the networked global order would be defined by flows of goods and services rather than power blocs, and by the rights of individuals rather than warring states. They sought to build a new world based on pooled sovereignty, mutually beneficial interdependence, and universal norms that led to a virtuous cycle, and which all would eventually accept. But rather than making power irrelevant, these networks have simply supplied new tools and techniques for exercising it.

In the age of unpeace power is exercised through control over flows of ideas, people, goods, money and data, and via the connections they establish. And in this world, we can see how the forces that were meant to bring the world together are now dividing it. To understand it properly we need to look deeper at the battlegrounds of the twenty-first century. We need to explore the anatomy of unpeace.

PART THREE:

WEAPONS AND WARRIORS

CHAPTER FIVE:

AN ANATOMY OF UNPEACE: HOW GLOBALIZATION WAS TURNED INTO A WEAPON

President Recep Tayyip Erdoğan is not the sort of man who likes to grovel. Born into a poor background as one of five children, he has the manner and persona of a street fighter. When he was a schoolboy he used to sell lemonade and sesame rolls on the streets, and funded his degree in business administration by playing semi-professional football. When he entered politics, as an Islamist he faced regular persecution. He once lost a job in the Istanbul Transport Authority for refusing his secularist boss's injunction to shave off his moustache. Erdoğan eventually ended up in prison in 1998 for inciting religious hatred after publicly reading an Islamic poem that included the lines: 'the mosques are our barracks, the domes our helmets, the minarets our bayonets and the faithful our soldiers . . .'[1] On the global stage, he has sought a reputation as the alpha male's alpha male – unafraid to pick fights with friend and foe alike.

When I went to see him, in the grandiose 1,000-room presidential complex that he built for himself at a reported cost of $615 million, he oozed confidence and treated me with the courtesy and charm of a sultan receiving tribute from a foreign guest.[2] He was funny and assertive, attacking Europe for its attitude to Muslims, the United States for its missteps in Syria, and telling stories about meetings with Nicolas Sarkozy and his wife Carla Bruni. But one topic he avoided was his relationship with the Russian President Vladimir Putin. Before I left he presented me with a tie monogrammed with his initials and he asked his photographer to capture a shot of us shaking hands. When they sent me the photo later I noted that it was deliberately taken from an angle which made the president tower above me against the gilded backdrop of his 'sultan's palace'.

One reason that Putin may not have been discussed was that earlier in that week – a few days before we met – President Erdoğan was forced to show a side of his personality that is usually hidden from view: humility and contrition. He had issued a statement apologizing to the Russian president. The background was a long-running dispute between Ankara and Moscow over the civil war in Syria. These two tough-man leaders had found themselves on different sides of the struggle – with Putin supporting President Assad and Erdoğan backing various rebel groups that were trying to overthrow him. As Moscow increased its military involvement in Syria, it began bombing rebel groups near the Turkish border, including several Turkomen groups that were backed by Ankara. The Turkish military protested against this many times in vain. Eventually, Erdoğan lost patience and gave the order in November 2015 to shoot down a Russian Sukhoi Su-24M fighter jet that had entered Turkish airspace. The image of the falling plane immediately went viral. Calls for revenge exploded across the Russian media and internet. Protesters hurled stones and eggs at the Turkish embassy in Moscow. The high-profile host of Russia's main political TV talk show compared the downing of the jet to the 1914 assassination of Archduke Franz Ferdinand that triggered the First

World War. So how did Russia's hawkish leader, Vladimir Putin, respond to the battle cries of his people?

He signed a decree halting fruit and vegetable imports from Turkey, banning charter flights and the sale of package holidays, and scrapped Russia's visa-free regime with the country.

By the time I met with President Erdoğan in August 2016, Vladimir Putin's counterattack had worked. The sanctions were brutally effective. In 2014, 3.3 million Russian tourists travelled to Turkey, but official figures released in June 2016 revealed a 92 per cent fall year-on-year in Russian visitors. Russia also used to be a major market for Turkish goods, ranging from vegetables to clothing to construction materials, as well as a source of remittances from Turkish workers and small entrepreneurs in Russia. In the first four months of 2016, bilateral trade plummeted to 45 per cent of the level it reached in the same period in 2015.[3] Estimates of the combined cost of Turkish losses from tourism, small-scale luggage trade, and official exports – from agriculture and steel products to textiles – were around $14–15 billion. That is why Erdoğan reached out to Moscow with an uncharacteristic apology for downing the plane and a request to patch up the relationship.

Putin is not shy of using military force. He has sent troops and weapons to Chechnya, Georgia, Ukraine, Syria and Libya. But in the conflict with Turkey, he showed that the most important battleground of conflict between great powers will not be the air or ground. Rather, it will be the interconnected infrastructure of the global economy: disrupting trade and investment, the movement of people, transport links, international law, and the internet. Of course what he did was not a uniquely Russian trick. Putin, in fact, knew how harmful sanctions could be to others because he himself had been the victim of EU and US embargoes after his annexation of Crimea two years earlier. He could see how each of the five global networks purporting to bring about peace could be transformed into a battleground.

ECONOMIC WARFARE

Sanctions, population expulsions and trade wars have been around for centuries but until the world became organized around global supply chains, and a dollarized financial system, it was hard to strangle foreign economies and societies at so little cost to oneself.[4] All types of economic activity – trade, finance, ideas and people – are now being used as weapons. It is an irony that it is the United States of America – the country that brought us the 'Dell Theory of Conflict Prevention' – that has done the most to turn the international trading and financial system into a battleground.

US sanctions used to be very blunt instruments – not unlike the Russian sanctions against Turkey – and they only used to work well on countries that were directly dependent on US markets. But, around the turn of the century, there was a revolution in American thinking which allowed the systematic weaponization of economic links, using cooperation with multinational companies, which gradually transformed the idea of sanctions from catch-all blockades such as the one they introduced against Cuba in the 1960s to finely targeted regimes that were applied towards Iran, North Korea and Russia. This new generation of network-savvy measures is to the Russian sanctions – in the parlance of the Pentagon – a scalpel to their sledgehammer.

The transformation of financial warfare was the work of an improbable warlord, the former Treasury official Stuart Levey. Levey, a fast-talking lawyer from Ohio, was the first ever Under Secretary of the Treasury for Terrorism and Financial Intelligence in the Bush administration. When he started work, he joined a team of self-styled 'guerrillas in grey suits' who had been following money trails and using the regulation of finance to pursue the global war on terror after the devastation of 9/11. As part of their fight they had gone after money-launderers, circulated lists of terrorists to banks and started introducing sanctions against countries suspected of producing weapons of mass destruction, such as North Korea and Iran.

The process of sanctioning Iran proved frustrating. The USA did not do much trade with Tehran, so American sanctions had a limited impact. Moreover, as soon as Levey thought they were making progress getting allies such as the European Union to cut their imports of oil and gas from Tehran, other powers such as China would step in and buy up any spare capacity. Eventually Levey realized that they would have more impact if they could get the private sector to do the work for them – and take advantage of the dominance of the dollar in the global financial system. His big idea was to get banks to refuse to have anything to do with Iran – and to use that as a way of strangling other forms of investment and commerce. While UN sanctions can always be circumvented or even vetoed, the dollar's unique position as a reserve and clearing currency in 87 per cent of all foreign exchange transactions allows the American government to dictate terms to every bank and company in the world.[5]

Levey's plan was a kind of blackmail: banks are only as reputable as their clients' practices, he would say, and Iran was backing terrorists and pursuing a nuclear programme. Levey launched an 'Iran financial road-show', meeting over one hundred times with bank officials around the world. Coupled with his quiet diplomacy were less quiet enforcement actions. In his first five years, dozens of banks were fined including Lloyds, Standard Chartered, Barclays, ABN Amro, Clearstream, ING Groep, HSBC Holdings and Credit Suisse Group before the most high-profile case against BNP Paribas, which was fined a stunning $8.5 billion.[6] An essential first step to make this campaign possible was asking SWIFT – a global information transfer service based in Brussels – whether the US Treasury could get access to its records to go after terrorist financing. The SWIFT data were described by a Treasury

official as the 'Rosetta stone' for US financial warfare. What started as a
war against al-Qaeda grew to encompass measures against North Korea,
Iran, Sudan, and even Russia. Once the Treasury had the data on financial transactions they used this to tighten a financial noose around
economies they disapproved of. They put enormous pressure on SWIFT
to disconnect banks from those countries, thereby shutting them off
from international credit.[7]

Once banks began to be fined billions of dollars, they had a strong
incentive to build a vast machinery employing thousands of people to
enforce the sanctions. A study by the British accounting firm Deloitte
found that over half of financial service institutes *outside of the US* explicitly use the sanctions list developed by the American Office of Foreign
Assets Control (OFAC) as the key list of whom to do business with.[8]

It took a while for people outside the United States to realize how
powerful what the CIA director of the time called a 'twenty-first-century
precision-guided munition' is.[9] When Vladimir Yakunin, Putin's close
friend and the head of Russian Railways, was put on the US sanctions
list he was very dismissive, declaring to the *Financial Times*, 'I did not
intend to travel to the US. I have no assets. So it does not bother me at
all.'[10] But as one analyst explained, the real threat is not the inconven-
ience of having assets frozen or a visa ban but the signal they send to
banks: 'They are the financial equivalent of leprosy, discouraging financial institutions from touching the targeted entity in any way.'[11] Once
you are targeted, it is not just US banks that refuse to deal with you, but
any entity which needs to have correspondent banks in the USA, which
is roughly everyone. That makes it very difficult for people on the list to
do anything – whether it is buying a chalet in Courchevel or paying
school fees in London. And today different parts of the American system are applying the scientific approach that they developed towards
banking to other parts of our connected economy. As trade and value
chains become so much more globalized, they have discovered that

hitting one small link in the chain – such as chips or semiconductors – can be enough to bring a company or country to its knees. China doesn't have the capacity to manufacture the crucial chips it needs to power its economy and imports roughly $300 billion of them every year. The USA is trying to squeeze it. As *The Economist* claims: 'In the 20th century the world's biggest economic choke-point involved oil being shipped through the Strait of Hormuz. Soon it will be silicon etched in a few technology parks in South Korea and Taiwan.'[12] This is the vulnerability the US government exploited in the measures it took to restrict exports to Chinese tech giants such as Huawei and ZTE from 2018. From vaccines and masks to cars and telephone handsets, the reliance on complex 'just-in-time' global supply chains with critical components supplied by only a few specialist players increasingly exposes different nations to the risk of geopolitical pressure.

Faced with war-weary publics and tightening budgets, Western states are projecting power through their influence over the global economy, trade and finance (including the dollar and euro), and through their control over multinational corporations domiciled in their countries. The USA, the European Union and the United Nations currently have sanctions in place against thirty-one different countries in five continents around the world. It has been interesting to watch these weapons being tried out on ever higher-value targets. They began using them on small and weak countries like North Korea and then scaled up their use on to Iran and then Russia. There is now the potential to use them against China, the second-biggest economy in the world. This is a huge leap, with potential costs for the US long-term position in the global financial system. That is a major reason why Treasury was the actor in US government most reluctant to go after the Chinese. But it is worth noting that anxiety about this happening spiked in China significantly last year when Chinese banks were forced to comply with US sanctions on Hong Kong officials.[13]

No other country yet benefits from the same network that the dollar gives the United States, but many are using techniques such as economic blockades (Turkey against Armenia), financial sanctions (South Korea against North Korea), travel and visa bans (China, South Korea, and Japan), gas cut-offs (Russia against its neighbours), restrictions in sales of rare earths (China against Japan), as well as aid suspension, increased import/export inspections, the closing of businesses and expropriation, and denying regulatory approvals and licences.[14] Often the most effective tools are to dangle carrots – loans, investments, new infrastructure – and then to threaten to withhold them, a favourite Chinese tactic. While non-Western countries are not reluctant to use economic warfare, they are more cautious to openly call it that. Often, measures are disguised as stricter sanitary controls or customs-related delays that just so happened to take place against entities from certain countries they have a political disagreement with.

Many states have begun to defend themselves from these develop-ments, aiming at decreasing their dependencies on other countries. Economic mercantilism is growing. 'Buy local' campaigns are often thinly veiled strategies to strengthen domestic producers against inter-national competition in order to make the state less dependent. China now explicitly aims at boosting its domestic technology sector and its domestic economic demand as a way to limit its vulnerability to Ameri-can pressure.[15] China is trying to build a digital currency that can challenge the dollar, a banking system that is insulated from the United States, and a series of foundational technologies that stop the United States from strangling its access to global markets. In 2020 China and Russia even talked about creating a 'financial alliance' to reduce their dependence on the dollar, as they shifted to doing the majority of their bilateral trade in euros and their national currencies (as recently as 2015 90 per cent of their transactions were in dollars).[16]

As it becomes successful at this many fear that Beijing could be tempted to use many of the same techniques that Washington has used – turning its global financial networks into tools of Chinese foreign policy. China has introduced new laws on the screening of foreign investment, promulgated a new export controls law, drawn up an 'unreliable entity' list, and adopted an EU-style statute blocking the extraterritorial jurisdiction of US law. People are increasingly complaining that, by using these techniques, Beijing is applying its writ against Hong Kong, in the South China Sea, along the Belt and Road, and in cyberspace.[17] The fear is that it could force users of its digital currency, its technologies or capital to follow Chinese sanctions in the same way that Washington has used its privileged position – but in support of authoritarianism rather than democratic aims. There are also some uniquely Chinese innovations such as building a 'social credit' scheme for companies that mirrors the one it introduced for citizens (see Chapter One). In the same way that citizens can be punished for behaving in ways that the Communist Party disapproves of, so too could companies be privileged or punished because of their loyalty to Beijing. So far China has used its market power to bully countries such as Australia, as well as other players like the NBA and Hollywood, but this points to a different agenda. Many fear it is deliberately building dependencies for international firms and foreign states so that it can impose its laws and priorities around the world.

Back in 1941 Albert Hirschman claimed that people were wrong to think that trade was simply motivated by profits and came up with a theory of 'power trading'. 'It is possible,' he wrote, 'to turn foreign trade into an instrument of power, of pressure, and even of conquest.'[18] Hirschman's insights came from studying how Germany manipulated the global trading system to degrade its adversaries' capabilities, entrap nations as reluctant allies, and build up its own industries under the Kaiser and the Nazis. Modern-day analysts claim that China is following many of the rules of so-called 'power trading': turning nations into dependent vassal states by creating vested interests in those countries, using monetary manipulation to reduce export costs, dumping products to prevent the industrialization of potential competitors, using industrial espionage to steal intellectual property, and targeting key industries for potential dominance.[19]

Although, on a human level, the fear of being blown to smithereens is much more visceral than the pain of regulations or tariffs, these connectivity weapons can hurt many *more* people than bombs. There are no comprehensive studies of how many lives have been blighted or ended by sanctions but there were clues in a series of studies of national sanctions regimes.

Some of the stories from places that have lived with sanctions, like North Korea, are heartbreaking: mothers so undernourished that they were unable to produce milk, people in the better-off parts eating their harvest before it was ripe, even horrific stories of people eating their own children.[20] Although many of the problems come from the inhumanity of the regimes that are targeted, there is no question that sanctions have blighted the lives of millions – from Venezuela and Iran to Sudan and North Korea – primarily by restricting access to food, medicines and electricity and by wreaking general economic havoc. Their social impact is often devastating. Prices for imports skyrocket; medicines become scarce; water quality decreases; jobs are lost; and public services like healthcare, sanitation and education decline. Ultimately, lots of people die avoidable deaths.

Studies have shown that sanctions typically reduce economic growth by about 2 per cent a year – so a country can lose a quarter of its economy after just a decade.[21] In Syria, sanctions contributed to the doubling of unemployment[22] and saw 80 per cent of the population plunged into poverty rates. In Iran, sanctions led the Iranian GDP to shrink by up to 10 per cent a year.[23] Venezuela already faced economic troubles before the introduction of the US sanctions but the IMF claimed that the sanctions led to inflation increasing to 500,000 per cent, while the percentage of Venezuelans living in extreme poverty went up to 85 per cent in 2018.[24] The political turmoil, socioeconomic instability and the on-going humanitarian crisis caused the largest external displacement crisis in Latin America's recent history.[25]

The health consequences are no less stark.[26] There was a big backlash against the human costs of catch-all sanctions in the 1990s. For example those placed on Iraq in the 1990s set back the health system by fifty years.[27] The infant mortality rate went back to levels not seen since the 1940s.[28] In Iraq, the UN estimated the number of deaths among children under five years during the sanctions in the 1990s at between 382,000 and 576,000. For these reasons, there was a move at the turn of the century to develop 'smart sanctions' targeted on elites rather than wider society.

But although the new generation of sanctions could theoretically be targeted on elites responsible for oppression or crimes against humanity, the trend of moving towards 'maximum pressure' is once again hurting entire societies. For example, Harvard University calculates that at least 4,000 people died in North Korea due to the sanctions and funding shortfalls in 2018.[29] US sanctions in Venezuela were credited with causing over 40,000 deaths in 2017 and 2018.[30] And many studies have argued that Iran's healthcare system as well as its economy has been decimated by Western sanctions. The same thing is true of Syria today, where British doctors working in Aleppo claim that 'over 80 per cent of those requiring urgent medical treatment die as a result of their injuries, or lack of basic care, medicine and equipment'.[31]

INFRASTRUCTURE COMPETITION

Hungary's prime minister built a reputation on saying no to migrants – particularly those who are not Christian. He introduced razor wire fences, invested in border guards, and broke EU law to keep foreigners out of Hungary. But there is one exception to his rule. In 2013, he introduced a 'residency bond' aimed at attracting wealthy Chinese into the country. Since then some 10,000 have settled in this Central European country, taking advantage of the clean air, schools and universities and the culture of this ancient land.[32] Viktor Orbán's motivation was not a desire to help Chinese connect with the culture of 'Mitteleuropa' – rather it was the desire to hitch Hungary's wagon to the Chinese economic juggernaut.

Orbán's goal was to turn Hungary into China's hub in Central and Eastern Europe. In the last five years, China has invested over $3 billion in Hungary, and bilateral trade turnover has grown to an annual $10 billion.[33] The aim was not just to get China to pour money into Hungary, but also to link it up with Chinese trade and communications routes. The Chinese prime minister and Viktor Orbán launched a flagship high-speed railway that will connect Budapest to Belgrade. And China's telecoms giant Huawei has been operating in Hungary for the past ten years, employing 2,500 people and drawing on the services of almost 600 local suppliers.[34] These investments are not simply about money (in fact China has put much less money into Hungary than it has into Poland and other western European countries). They also represent an ideological escape route from the West's traditions of liberal democracy.

Viktor Orbán first came to prominence as a 26-year-old activist for liberal values. On 16 June 1989, he gave a rousing speech in Heroes' Square, Budapest, demanding free elections and the withdrawal of Soviet troops. The occasion was the reburial of Imre Nagy and the martyrs of the 1956 Hungarian Revolution. Overnight he became one of the most articulate and effective advocates of the 'return to Europe', founding a political party committed to liberalism and rising to the premiership of his country at the tender age of thirty-five. After four years in power, he lost the elections and spent almost a decade in opposition during which he totally transformed his worldview.

When Orbán came back to power in 2010, his political project was about escaping from, rather than embracing, Europe. The erstwhile liberal reinvented himself as the biggest enemy of his previous philosophy. He rapidly set about centralizing power, reintroducing state planning and protectionism. And with an iconic speech at Băile Tuşnad in Romania (Tusnádfürdő) on 26 July 2014, he crystallized his ideas. 'A trending topic in thinking,' he said, 'is understanding systems that are not Western, not liberal, not liberal democracies, maybe not even democracies, and yet making nations successful. Today, the stars of international analyses are Singapore, China, India, Turkey, Russia . . . We are searching for . . . ways of parting with Western European dogmas, making ourselves independent from them . . . in this great world-race.'[35]

It is striking how many countries who once queued up for EU membership are now trying to curry favour with China. Beijing's leaders have identified the second battleground of the age of unpeace: competition through the physical infrastructure of globalization. Many countries have understood that if they cannot be independent, the next best thing is to make their partners dependent on them. If all roads lead to Rome, countries are best served by becoming Rome. This quest for 'asymmetric interdependence' is encouraging leading regional powers – Russia, Germany, Brazil, South Africa, and Nigeria – to try to entrench their role as core economies. But few countries have taken the 'road' element of the saying as literally as China.

In 2013, President Xi Jinping announced the 'One Belt, One Road' project – later rebranded as the 'Belt and Road Initiative' (BRI) – intended to link China to cities as far away as Bangkok and Budapest, and develop the Eurasian coast. The original promise of the Belt and Road Initiative was to link sixty-five countries and markets, with China as the hub around which all the contact flows. China has promised to invest $1 trillion – roughly seven times as much as the Marshall Plan.[36] 'For a great power to rise, it needs the support of its periphery,' the Chinese nationalist thinker Yan Xuetong argues. The BRI is the most ambitious of China's infrastructure projects aimed at exporting China's surplus capacity while expanding its access to raw materials and export markets. That China has perfected infrastructure diplomacy should not come as a surprise: with over 160 Chinese cities boasting populations of more than one million (Europe has thirty-five) it has had to learn to build more infrastructure faster than any other power in history.

China's approach to international integration through infrastructure is very different from the EU's. The EU has also built infrastructure across the continent and with its neighbours, but its goal was always to try to bury power politics. Germany, in particular, was keen to use regional integration to assuage the fears of its neighbours. Berlin has struggled with a sense that the creation of the euro and the infrastructure for global supply chains has led other countries to feel that they are reduced to its periphery (as we explored in Chapter Three). But China, on the other hand, seems to see the projection of power as one of the explicit goals of its new infrastructure projects. It uses offers of infrastructure and aid to buy political loyalty and favours.[37] These efforts are worrying many of Beijing's neighbours, who fear that China's Belt and Road project creates dependencies that can then be exploited. On the one hand is the fear of debt diplomacy – where China lends huge amounts of money to countries to build infrastructure and then demands political concessions when they inevitably struggle to repay. The cost of the railway between China and Laos represents 80 per cent of Laos's annual budget, leaving the country very dependent on Chinese support.[38] There are also more traditional security fears: that the transport containers full of shoes and T-shirts could as easily send tanks and soldiers from China into the continent. There are still residual memories across Asia of Japanese railway transports during the Second World War.[39]

As Covid-19 raged across the world and many economies were

plunged into crisis, China's infrastructure projects also ran into trouble. Some states struggled to meet their debt payments and Chinese institutions paused their lending.[40] As it navigates a developing world debt crisis Beijing will no doubt reassess its approach to political and economic risk, but Xi Jinping's signature project is seen as a generational one. What is more, even as the physical infrastructure projects are paused, Beijing is refocusing its energy on the digital side of the Belt and Road as we will see below.[41]

Hungary's strategy of binding itself to China is part of a search for geopolitical options. Orbán would rather be a small 'core' than rely on his country's position as part of Europe's large 'periphery'. By joining China's sphere of influence, he thinks he can counterbalance Germanic influences. But although he probably has very little to fear from Chinese troops, he may end up losing sovereignty as he drifts into a Chinese periphery.

WEAPONIZING THE DIGITAL WORLD

If infrastructure is being weaponized in the traditional economy, the internet has been the front line of the new tech wars. In just a few years the internet has gone from being seen as the ultimate unifier of a global village to being seen as 'the perfect weapon'.[42] There are several tech wars being waged between China and America which are turning the technology of connectivity into one that is dividing the world.

The first is a battle over cybersecurity, where America's National Security Agency is up against the Chinese Ministry of Public Security. Second, there is a tussle for primacy between corporate superpowers that pits US tech giants (Google, Apple, Facebook, Amazon, Microsoft) against China's new titans (Baidu, Alibaba, Tencent and Xiaomi). This conflict includes both hardware (chips, 5G, etc.) and software (AI, algorithms, data). It governs the flow of ideas, intellectual property and patents. A third battle over the rules of engagement has balkanized the internet into different worlds. And as time goes on these tussles are becoming entangled – and leading to ever more fragmentation, conflict and 'unpeace'.

It used to be that there were 'good' and 'bad' guys and 'fair' and 'unfair' competition. Everybody knew the rules. But now that is changing. The science and technology that united the world in the past is becoming the most divisive realm of the future. Just look at the story of these two tech leaders, a man called Zhu Hua and a woman named Wu Xifeng.

Zhu Hua likes to go by the hacker name of God Killer, but the grainy photographs of him on the FBI's 'most wanted' page give him a somewhat less than Nietzschean appearance. His chubby face and porcine features are scrunched up in different poses; in one he is snapped shovelling food into his open mouth. The FBI claims he is as greedy for data as for junk food – squirrelling away hundreds of gigabytes of sensitive information over a twelve-year period. That is why they made the rare move of taking him to court. The Grand Jury of the Southern District of New York indicted him for 'conspiracy to commit computer intrusion, wire fraud and aggravated identity theft'.[43]

Zhu is alleged to be a leading member of a hacking group that has gone under the names of 'Stone Panda', 'Red Apollo', 'Cloud Hopper' and 'Potassium' among others. Its members claim to work for a company in Tianjin, a second-tier megacity 80 km south of Beijing, but the FBI thinks this is a front for the Chinese Ministry of State Security.[44] Stone Panda's hacking activities cover a wide spectrum of mischief, and their escapades are respected for their sophistication and audacity.

The grand jury indictment accuses Zhu of stealing intellectual property from at least forty-five commercial and defence technology companies in Brazil, Canada, Finland, France, Germany, India, Japan,

Sweden, Switzerland, the United Arab Emirates, the United Kingdom and the United States. He is also accused of compromising the computer systems of the United States Department of the Navy and of stealing the personal information of more than 100,000 navy personnel (almost a third of the combined staff). Most of the sectors he snooped on – aviation, space, satellites, manufacturing, oil and gas exploration, computer processors – lie at the heart of the Chinese government's industrial plans. 'More than 90 per cent of the department's cases alleging economic espionage over the past seven years involve China,' said former Deputy Attorney General Rod Rosenstein at a press conference detailing the indictment. 'More than two-thirds of the department's cases involving thefts of trade secrets are connected to China.'[45]

The US government knows a thing or two about surveillance. Edward Snowden has shown how the US National Security Agency turned the internet into a gigantic snooper's charter. The most important infrastructure is the network of fibre-optic cables that connect the world. Roughly 97 per cent of intercontinental traffic goes through just 300 cables.[46] After 9/11, the US established the 'STELLARWIND' programme to suck up data going through US networks. As General Michael Hayden, the head of the NSA, said, 'This is a home game for us. Are we not going to take advantage that so much of it goes through Redmond, Washington? Why would we not turn the most powerful telecommunications and computing management structure on the planet to our use?' He was referring to the headquarters of Microsoft, but his activities also targeted AT&T and in fact managed to collect data directly from the cables – making it unnecessary to even ask permission from companies.[47]

The FBI's worries are not restricted to theft of intellectual property and surveillance – they worry about threats to lives and security. They know how much damage cyber attacks such as the Stuxnet worm we saw in Chapter Four can inflict. And so they are very worried about falling victim to attacks themselves. Even economically motivated attacks can kill accidentally. For example, the Russian ransomware 'WannaCry' attack in May 2017 was designed to extract money from companies, but as a by-product of its success it ended up disabling much of the British National Health Service's electronic infrastructure. It resulted in almost 20,000 cancelled appointments, 600 GP surgeries having to return to pen and paper, and five hospitals simply diverting ambulances, unable to handle any more emergency cases.[48]

These days there is as much attention on politics and psychology as on physical infrastructure. The USA has been obsessed with Russia's attempts to hack the 2016 presidential elections (a campaign known as 'Grizzly Steppe') as well as the fake news factories Moscow supported to spew out political misinformation. But Chinese groups like Stone Panda had been at work at similar operations before then, launching high-profile cyber attacks on the Commission on Elections in the Philippines in March 2016 (where it stole the details of 70 million voters) as well as on China-sceptic parties in Japan and Taiwan.[49] Since 2016, there have been attempts to interfere with national elections in twenty countries, representing 1.2 billion people.[50] Although many hacks were not particularly effective at their explicit aim they often achieved the broader target of making the democratic population fearful of interference and mistrustful of the results. In some cases the spread of disinformation can undermine the idea of truth itself.

Western societies feel increasingly vulnerable to multi-layered attacks. American cyber experts warn that individuals or small groups could take down the entire US electrical grid, incapacitate the UK's Trident nuclear submarine fleets or convulse the banking industry. And the use of disinformation could spread panic in an already rattled country.[51]

But what happened to the other tech leader, Wu Xifeng, is maybe even more consequential for the digital competition of the future. Professor Wu was seeking to find a cure for cancer rather than spreading viruses on American computers. She had worked twenty-seven of her fifty-six years at the University of Texas's MD Anderson Cancer Center, where she was director of the Center for Public Health and Translational Genomics. She was a naturalized US citizen and a model researcher with a publication list of 540 papers. The international cooperation she pioneered – including with universities and hospitals in her native China – was regarded as an embodiment of MD Anderson's mission to 'end cancer in Texas, America and the world'. But her approach came from the world of yesterday and fell foul of the new rules of engagement. No one accused her of stealing anyone's ideas. Her crime was to 'secretly aid and abet cancer research in China'. Although no formal charge was made – and no proof presented of her having given China any proprietary information – Wu was placed on unpaid leave while she was being investigated. In the end she quietly resigned her post in January 2020.

Ways of working that were encouraged for decades are now being criminalized. FBI agents read private emails and submit ethnically Chinese researchers to loyalty tests, even arresting them at airports. The philosophy behind the new approach was set out by FBI director Christopher Wray, who claimed that Chinese intelligence services use every tool at their disposal – including state-owned businesses, students, researchers, and ostensibly private companies – to rob intellectual property.[52] 'China seems determined to steal its way up the economic ladder, at our expense,' he said, and alleged that whereas the Cold War was fought by armies and governments, the new contest is being waged, on China's side, by the whole of society. The USA now needs its own 'whole-of-society' response, he claimed. In today's Washington DC, worries have shifted from illegal hacking to the legal catch-up by China in areas such as 5G, artificial intelligence, quantum computing and blockchain.

There is also a lot of concern about the way that China is using the digital silk road to export many of its technologies and to shape global standards and norms.[53] Beijing has been inspired by the

nineteenth-century German industrialist Werner von Siemens' claim
that 'he who owns the standards, owns the market'. As a result it has sent
top officials to take up the leadership of global standard-setting bodies
such as the International Telecommunications Union (ITU), the International Organization for Standardization (ISO) and the International
Electrotechnical Commission (IEC).[54] As of 2019 China has also reached
eighty-five standardization agreements with forty-nine countries and
regions.[55] When I was in Pakistan in 2019, I heard that the government
was implementing a 'safe cities' project to introduce facial recognition
and surveillance in the top big cities, an initiative that had been subcon-
tracted to Chinese companies like SenseTime and its rivals. The Chinese
government has exported its AI and surveillance technology to many
countries around the world – from Azerbaijan to Zimbabwe. Further-
more, it has hosted media officials from thirty-six countries to
three-week seminars on its sprawling system of censorship and surveillance. And, according to Freedom House, around forty countries have
commissioned Chinese companies to build their telephone infrastructure. The fear is that many countries will combine the use of Chinese
technology with a vision of a 'managed internet' that prohibits free
speech and keeps data in the country to allow the government to use it
for surveillance.[56]

Long imagined as a cross-border, non-territorial global online com-
mons, the internet is already becoming a maze of national or regional
and often conflicting rules. Academics have identified several competing organizing philosophies for the internet.[57] The original founders in
Silicon Valley favoured an open internet with transparent standards and
portable technology. But today it is competing with a Chinese internet
where technologies of surveillance and identification help ensure social
cohesion and security by targeting would-be criminals, terrorists or dis-
senters. The US attitude to the internet has evolved, and is now mainly
commercial, treating online data as a commodity to be monetized while

excluding others from using it. In contrast, Europeans are trying to create a 'bourgeois internet' which minimizes trolling and bad behaviour
by offering strict privacy laws. Another philosophy – led by Russia – is
of the internet as the soft underbelly of rival nations, which can be
exploited for disinformation and hacking.

WEAPONS OF MASS MIGRATION

'You are not the ones who picked up the body of the Aylan baby, nor the
ones feeding the three million refugees,' said Recep Tayyip Erdoğan to the
then EU Commission president in the middle of the migration crisis of
2015. 'You freaked out when there were fifty thousand refugees at the border and said, "What if Turkey opens the gates?" Look at me now. If you go
any further, these borders will open.'[58] Erdoğan saw the 3 million desperate refugees who had come to Turkey as a bargaining chip to increase his
power over its neighbours. In a Machiavellian game of politics he reportedly threatened to open the borders and ship the refugees by bus into the
EU unless they acceded to his demands.[59] The Turkish president successfully pressured the EU into agreeing to a refugee deal that earned Turkey
€6 billion, visa liberalizations and steps towards EU membership.

Erdoğan is not the first politician to use migrants and refugees in this
type of blackmail. Migration experts have identified over seventy-five
attempts to instrumentalize migration flows since the 1951 Refugee
Convention came into force, more than one per year.[60] The number of
refugees used in such moves ranges from a few thousand (Polish asylum
seekers in 1994) to over 10 million (east Pakistanis in 1971). Libyan
strongman Muammar Gaddafi famously threatened to 'turn Europe
black' if it did not pay him €4 billion to hold back migrants travelling to
Europe in 2010.[61] (Gaddafi had successfully used this tool in 2004, 2006
and 2008 and it was used again by Libyan warlords after he was deposed.)

It is no wonder that Gaddafi used this threat several times – research shows that the weaponization of migration is a particularly effective tool. In nearly three-quarters of these historical cases, the coercers achieved at least some of their articulated objectives, and in over half they achieved everything they sought, making this instrument of state-level influence more effective than war or sanctions.[62] Migration is a particularly effective weapon for the weak against the strong. There is no way that countries like Cuba, Haiti, or Mexico could threaten the USA with military force. Their demographic time bombs have been more persuasive than real bombs could ever have been.[63]

Global migration has almost tripled in the past fifty years.[64] There are now some 240 million people living outside their country of birth – enough to form the fifth-biggest state in the world.[65] Some states have realized the potential of instrumentalizing it, turning the gateways of migration into a source of power. They have developed different approaches as 'Generators', 'New Colonialists', 'Go-betweens', and 'Integrators'.

The first group, *Generators*, actively engineer migration to use it as a weapon. During the Syrian war, the US General Philip Breedlove – who served as Supreme Allied Commander Europe in NATO – accused Russia of using its deliberate bombing of hospitals and other civilian centres in Syria to drive refugees into Europe.[66] Russia has also used the large number of people from the post-Soviet states who live in it to blackmail their countries of origin. For example it threatened to restrict visas for the millions of settlers from Tajikistan (who sent large remittances back home) if their government refused to join Moscow's Eurasian Economic Union in 2014.[67] In a much less violent manner, the former British Prime Minister Theresa May obliquely threatened the EU with 3 million repatriates, in the Brexit negotiations, by not initially guaranteeing the right to remain for EU migrants in the UK.

The second category, *New Colonialists*, encourage their own populations to emigrate and flex their geopolitical muscles through these human ties.[68] Just as settlers from Europe spread across the world to the benefit of their homelands in the eighteenth and nineteenth centuries, the most mobile citizens of the twenty-first century are helping their countries of origin to get access to markets, technology and a political voice beyond their borders. For example, there are tens of millions in the Chinese diaspora around the world, and over a million who have settled in Africa alone. And when some of those migrants return to China, the skills and knowledge they have picked up are expertly harvested – as we saw with the ex-Microsoft staff at SenseTime. Called 'sea turtles', these returning migrants dominate China's technology industry.

The other continent-sized country, India, also has a diaspora of about 20 million Indian citizens who are extremely successful and hyper-connected. One in ten companies in Silicon Valley is set up by Indian-born entrepreneurs. Google and Microsoft's chief executives are Indian, as are the inventor of the Intel Pentium processor and the chief technology officer at Motorola. How does this benefit India? For one, India gets $58 billion in remittances every year, the highest number worldwide and almost 4 per cent of its GDP, more than it spends on education. And while it is impossible to prove a causal connection, the influx of Indians into America also coincided with a shift in both countries' geopolitical orientation. The historic deal which saw the US recognize New Delhi's nuclear ambitions in 2005 marked the end of its policy of equidistance between India and Pakistan.

The third group are *Go-betweens*, like President Erdoğan. These are countries that use their geography to extract concessions from migration-phobic neighbours. They don't create migration flows themselves but exert power by opening and closing borders as it suits them. Cuba has taken on this role with the United States several times in recent history, most famously during the Mariel boatlift of 1980, during which 125,000 Cubans reached Florida (a number of whom had been released from prisons and mental health institutions). Niger – a major transit hub through which 90 per cent of all West African migrants pass on their way to Italy – succeeded in extracting €600 million from the last EU aid budget. Go-betweens' power usually appears suddenly, but they are at the mercy of geography and have little control over the timing of their power surge.

The fourth group are the *Integrators*. These are at the receiving end of migration flows and know how to use them to their advantage. For all the anti-migrant rhetoric in the twenty-first century, migrants are major drivers of global productivity, particularly in developed economies. Migrants create $7 trillion per year – almost 10 per cent of global GDP – even though they only represent 3.4 per cent of the world's population.[69] By moving to more productive regions and occupations, migrants contribute more to global GDP than they would have in their country of origin. Much more would be possible. McKinsey estimates that up to $1 trillion additional annual output would be possible through better integration in destination countries.[70] There is a huge economic dividend for countries that get integration right, a McKinsey Global Institute report notes.[71]

Libraries have been filled with accounts of how the United States has benefited from its ability to transform the brightest and the best from around the world into American citizens. Angola and Brazil have now reversed the brain drain and are receiving large flows of immigration from their former colonial power, Portugal.

But the two most eye-catching experiments in integration in recent times are in the Middle East: Israel and the so-called Islamic State (IS). Israel is the only country whose population has multiplied by nine in the space of fifty years. It is probably the first country to have a word – 'Aliyah' – for migrating to it. This is supported by a government infrastructure of 'Aliyah consultants' offering free one-way flights, language classes and practical support. A book that showed how Israel has reinvented itself as a digital 'start-up nation' asks the question: 'How is it that Israel – a country of 7.1 million people, only sixty years old, surrounded by enemies, in a constant state of war since its founding, with no natural resources – produces more start-up companies than large, peaceful, and stable nations like Japan, China, India, Korea, Canada, and the United Kingdom?'[72] The answer is immigration.

Neither would be happy with the parallel, but before it was bombed out of existence, IS's rapid emergence on the map drew many lessons from the Israeli example. It has also adopted a word for migrating to it – 'Hijra' – an Arabic word meaning 'emigration', evoking the prophet Muhammad's historic escape from Mecca, where assassins were plotting to kill him, to Medina. The so-called Islamic State may not have been recognized by anyone as an actual state, and it was eventually defeated militarily, but for many months it was one of the most successful receivers of migration. According to the Soufan Group, between 27,000 and 31,000 people travelled to Syria and Iraq from eighty-six countries[73] – and that is before you count all the groups around the region that declared loyalty to it, not to mention individuals in Western capitals who have claimed to be inspired by it. Against all the odds, IS was able to create a functional proto-state (complete with flag, currency, administrative structures, police); to enlarge and defend a large amount of territory (IS ruled at some point over more than 34,000 square miles[74]); to generate income (taxes, exporting oil, extortion, etc.) and to encourage more migrants to come (through the use of 'celebrity' fighters, propaganda videos and social media).[75] That it managed to survive for so long – in spite of the fact that it had united the USA, Russia, Iran, Israel and Saudi Arabia against it – was surprising.

The migration superpowers have had a huge impact on global economics and politics. The richest countries that first benefited from the globalization of trade have clubbed together in a group called the 'G7'. But another batch of countries outside the G7 – China, India, Israel,

Libya, Niger, Russia, and Turkey – have used migration to increase their clout. They could be called the 'M7'. Emigration, immigration, and control over the flow of people are now currencies of power. States that follow the M7's lead and adapt to this new age could supersize their geopolitical heft.

LAWFARE

In a connected world, we have no option but to work together to solve problems like climate change. What, after all, is more connected than the air we breathe, the water we drink and the climate we live in? There is as yet no 'Planet B', in spite of the best efforts of the super-rich to explore space travel. The big hope for globalists everywhere has been that climate change will shock national leaders out of their petty competition and instead focus their minds on protecting the future of the planet.

In 2018 the teenage activist Greta Thunberg sprang into the world like an envoy from the future with a warning about the suicidal course the world is set on.[76] The school strikes she started at the age of fifteen were a model for others all around the world as well as for new activist movements such as 'Extinction Rebellion'. In order to avoid the destruction of humanity, she urges us to focus on the fate of the planet as a whole, rather than on the relative performance of individual countries. She wants carbon-reduction deals to be governed by international law rather than the power of individual nations. And she cares about scientific truths rather than political slogans. Thunberg distilled the argument for global governance into a new political philosophy. Where global survival is at stake there can be no space for national interests or power games. The only distributional struggle she recognizes is between the old people who run the earth and the young who will inherit it.

There are no shades of grey – only fact and fiction, action and inaction. The world is on fire, she explains, and we need to act now in order to save it.

International law was intended to be a way of peacefully settling disputes between discordant nations. After the Cold War, multilateral institutions were supposed to be the benign invigilators of a new era of 'win-win' cooperation. But security experts have since come to regard international law as a weapon against hostile countries – they have nicknamed it 'lawfare' – while the institutions designed to administer it are becoming an important front for geopolitical competition.

There are many examples of countries undermining the international system by gridlocking institutions or pushing for a selective application of the rules. Emerging powers such as India, Russia and China have sought to frustrate the established powers by disrupting their use of existing institutions – from supporting well-known human rights abusers for election to the UN's Human Rights Council, to blocking the WTO's Doha Round of trade talks, or stopping the Organization for Security and Co-operation in Europe (OSCE) from conducting independent election observation missions. At other times they have even ignored their edicts, as Russia did over the 'open skies' agreement or China over the territorial rulings of the International Court of Justice in the South China Sea.

Emerging powers claim – although this is contested in Western capitals – that this behaviour has been mirrored by the United States and its allies, which have increasingly sought exceptions from the rules for themselves. For example, Washington calls on other countries to abide by the law of the sea, although it has not itself ratified the relevant UN convention. The EU and the US talk about the inviolability of borders and national sovereignty, but tried to change both norms through their intervention in Kosovo (which they tried to retroactively legitimate by coining the 'responsibility to protect').

As these universal institutions have become gridlocked, many countries have begun to work around them. There is a global trend towards forming competing, exclusive 'mini-lateral' groupings, rather than inclusive, universal multilateral projects. These groupings, bound by common values – or at least common enmities – are made up of like-minded countries at similar levels of development.

Frustrated by Chinese and Russian vetoes on everything from trade to human rights, the West began creating new groupings outside the universal institutions – such as the Trans-Pacific Partnership (TPP) in Asia and the Transatlantic Trade and Investment Partnership (TTIP) – that exclude Beijing and Moscow. In parallel to the Western order-building projects, Moscow and Beijing began to craft a 'world without the West' with a new set of groupings that include the BRICS (Brazil, Russia, India, China and South Africa), the Eurasian Economic Union (EEU) and Regional Comprehensive Economic Partnership (RCEP), as well as a host of sub-regional bodies. China has worked to promote parallel institutions to the Western-created ones – such as the Asian Infrastructure Investment Bank (AIIB) and the Shanghai Cooperation Organization (SCO) – some of which complement the existing order and some of which compete with it. These new friendship groups often struggle to agree very much, but their existence serves to weaken the legitimacy of global institutions.

Rather than embodying a new consensus, Greta Thunberg's speeches were assaulted by leaders such as Donald Trump, Jair Bolsonaro and Scott Morrison. Instead of treating action on climate change as a common project to save the planet, these leaders have tried to weaponize it to help their own economies while punishing others. If they deploy these weapons at international climate conferences, they risk derailing the entire negotiations. The giants of the Global South – countries like China, India, and Brazil – are now in absolute terms the world's biggest emitters. But they still have relatively low emissions per capita and point out that the developed economies have been the top carbon emitters for over a century. At the same time, the developed world is not willing to face up to fundamental changes in its way of life. Leaders like Australia's Scott Morrison have resorted to climate-change denial to avoid their responsibilities; in the face of national wildfires in January 2020 that burned 46 million acres and affected nearly 3 billion animals, reportedly among the 'worst wildlife disasters in modern history', Morrison went on holiday to Hawaii.[77]

Although Trump has departed – and Biden has rejoined the Paris Agreement – he was more of a symptom than a cause of the change in the climate negotiations. In the brief period of Greta Thunberg's life, the world has gone in exactly the opposite direction from her political doctrine: power has triumphed over law, politics over science and nationalism over internationalism. The Kyoto Protocol which was signed in 1992 had many flaws but it was broadly in line with Greta's recipe for survival: a multilateral treaty, with legally binding international targets, determined by the world's best scientists. But Kyoto was like a grape that withered on the vine. And the Paris Agreement of 2016, the best hope for a successor, represents a very different approach. It was hailed as a triumph only because hopes of getting a global agreement were so low. The reality is that it is much less constraining and intrusive than the Kyoto Protocol, which held national governments to commitments bound by international law. The Paris Agreement, on the other hand, left all the big countries free to adopt the national energy policies they had already decided on, while pretending that they had made a deal to tackle the climate emergency together. Meanwhile the planet burns.

Since the first global intergovernmental meetings on climate in 1988, global CO_2 emissions have risen by 40 per cent. The planet has already warmed by 1°C since we began burning coal on an industrial scale – and it could rise four times that amount by the end of the century.[78] Over half the world's rainforests have been chopped down since the 1960s.[79]

Half of the Great Barrier Reef has been bleached into an underwater grave by rising water temperatures. And the United Nations warns about the 'sixth mass extinction' which could wipe out over a million species of plants and animals.[80]

All this risks making Thunberg an envoy from a future that will never be. The softness of the Paris climate deal in relation to Kyoto is emblematic of a more profound hollowing out of international treaties over the last fifteen years. The same logic of non-binding agreements lies at the heart of the UN's Sustainable Development Goals and its Global Compact for Migration. Maybe most worrying is the way this approach is being exported to areas such as nuclear weapons, as successive arms control treaties are discarded.[81]

Connectivity, it seems, encourages some citizens and states to think about their own relative interests rather than focus on the welfare of the whole. The technology of connectivity was embraced by a globalized economy, powered by footloose capital with a logic of growth, expansion, and accumulation. This created huge concentrations of wealth and poverty which make cooperation difficult, because working for common interests results in asymmetrical rewards. Once this is overlaid with the psychology of envy unleashed by social media it becomes even harder to get citizens to focus on the common good rather than their relative situation in a global pecking order. One of the most dramatic examples of this was the online (dis)information campaign against the UN Global Compact for Migration that led to political crises in several European governments – Belgium, Estonia, Slovakia – and a decision to withdraw from the deal by almost twenty countries.[82]

The loss of control that comes from connectivity has also damaged faith in the power of government. Most people are aware that global problems cannot be solved alone. These feelings of powerlessness often lead to cynicism about the possibility of *any* solution emerging – what economists call 'collective action problems'. All too often, leaders and citizens conclude that the most rational short-term strategy is to do nothing oneself and hope that others will solve the crisis.

THE TIES THAT BREAK

With the collapse of the Soviet Union at the end of 1991, a divided world living in the shadow of the bomb gave way to a world of interconnection and interdependence. For some, it heralded the end of history, as a largely united world pursued the benefits of globalization. But contrary to the widespread hopes of the time, burgeoning connections between countries did not eradicate the tensions between them. The power struggles of the geopolitical era persisted, but in a new form.

This chapter has shown how trade wars, tariffs, sanctions and regulatory competition have weaponized the world's economic links. Our new physical and virtual global infrastructure enables countries to compete with each other by increasing their links to other countries – while denying contact to their rivals. Worldwide movements of people are also a source of power, as some countries leverage refugee flows or mobilize their diasporas overseas. Even international law has been turned into a weapon, as rival states manipulate it to achieve political goals rather than using it to limit their confrontations.

The forces binding people together have become battlegrounds, and each power has a different strategy for fighting in our new age of unpeace.

CHAPTER SIX:

THE NEW TOPOGRAPHY
OF POWER

Many fairy stories start with the words 'Once upon a time', but for most of history there was no commonly agreed idea of time. In fact, global time zones are one of the most revolutionary modern inventions. For most of human existence, people might as well have lived in different galaxies. Civilizations rose and fell. They had their own languages, cultures, religions, social mores, technologies and little or no contact with each other. In some ways, the story of humanity is an account of the gradual creation of one world. Around 10,000 BC, Earth was home to thousands of self-contained worlds. By 2000 BC they had consolidated into a few hundred and by AD 1415 – with the onset of European colonialism – it had become a few dozen.[1] The possibility that there could be any kind of 'global consciousness' only emerged in the second half of the nineteenth century.[2] Before that, the 'known world' in many continents stretched only a few miles inland from the coast.[3] But within the course of a few years all countries were explored, mapped and locked into a single global system through industry and empire. The period from 1850 to 1914 saw a wave of travel, trade and conquest which shrunk, connected and standardized the world – making it possible for the first time ever to apprehend the planet in its entirety. And one of the most important foundations for this was the unification of time.[4]

Before the world agreed on a 'standard time', the clocks on church towers, town halls and train stations in every city, town and village in Europe and North America were set according to the passage of the sun. In 1875, seventy-five railway times were used in the United States: six in St Louis, five in Kansas City and three in Chicago.[5] Even in the mid-nineteenth century, the idea of universal standardized time was still a utopian political project, advanced by idealists and eccentrics. Sandford Fleming (1827–1915) was a Scottish-Canadian administrator, engineer and inventor who designed Canada's first postage stamp, created a vast body of surveys and maps, and engineered much of the Intercolonial and Canadian Pacific Railways. But his most enduring achievement was the creation of worldwide standard time. In 1876, after missing a train in Ireland because of confusion about the time-table, he began writing a series of papers and pamphlets calling for a single way of measuring time, which he believed would be the prelude to the emergence of a world united by trade, technology and mutual understanding.[6] Fleming was a delegate at the International Meridian Conference in Washington DC in 1884, which translated his idealistic dream into an international treaty, and settled on a single, unified 'world time'. It took years for these ideas to be implemented, but by the end of the nineteenth century they had achieved unstoppable momentum. Time was not only standardized, but also democratized through cheap pocket watches, which became almost as ubiquitous as mobile phones today. The historian Jürgen Osterhammel has documented in intricate detail how these technologies led to the birth of the modern world and spawned the creation of a series of global networks of trade, communications, travel and ideas.[7]

If the long nineteenth century was a period when the world came together, the short twentieth century was defined by a logic of division. But when the Soviet Union collapsed in 1991, a second wave of connectivity could begin, facilitated by a revolution in information and communications technology that was almost as significant as the invention of the steam engine and the telegram. As a result, we're linked today in ways that Sandford Fleming could never have dreamed of. Half of the planet is now connected by smartphones and the internet into a single human-made network. And if the unification of time enabled countries to become linked, the unification of information has the potential to exponentially thicken our networks of connection, almost obliterating the distinction between home and abroad.

If Sandford Fleming was one of the most effective pamphleteers and campaigners for the first era of connectivity, the equivalent for the second era is the journalist Thomas Friedman, whose knack for reducing complex ideas to simple concepts has led millions of people to buy his paeans to globalization. At the beginning of the millennium Friedman's *The World Is Flat* was a bestselling book and on every businessperson's list.[8] His book looked at the ten forces that were flattening the world – from supply chains to wireless communications. And once they had levelled the global economy, Friedman told us, we should expect a frictionless level playing field.

But in fact, globalization created winners (up) and losers (down) within countries and across them. It reshaped the topography of individual countries and of the international system in a way that leaves us in a much more complex world. The world we are inhabiting today is not just round but mountainous too. To understand its topography we need to spend some time looking at the theory of networks.

HOW NETWORKS UNITE AND DIVIDE THE WORLD

Political scientists, economists, pollsters and international relations experts have developed models for understanding the world that focus on the individual incentives and powers of voters, consumers, statesmen and diplomats. But these models are increasingly unable to explain the ways of a world connected into a single networked system.

How many predicted the global financial crisis, the Arab uprisings, Brexit, the election of Trump? How many foresaw the collapse of newspapers, the rise of Uber, or Airbnb? And how many anticipated the way governments and people would react to Covid-19? But most importantly, how many thought that all of these upheavals would take place within a single decade? The sort of political upsets that are meant to happen once in a century seem to be happening every fifteen minutes.

A lot of the unpredictability in our economies, technological systems, politics and society stems from how they organize themselves. If the industrial era was defined by the hierarchies of factories, armies, churches and bureaucracies, the most powerful organizational form of our connected age is the network. A network is a fancy name for describing a collection of objects (nodes) which are connected by links (ties). It does not typically have a single centre but rather a series of connections between the nodes. However, some nodes are much more connected than others, bringing lots of separate networks together (hubs).[9]

Networks have existed as long as people have but for centuries they were outgunned by the deadly efficiency of hierarchies until technology emerged that could allow them to thrive. As we have seen, the digital revolution and globalization – coupled with the relative peace of the post-Cold War era – have seen the emergence of new networks of exchange that have wiped out some of the borders between countries and linked them together in new ways. The key feature of our age is that many of the institutions that used to be free-standing have reinvented themselves as nodes in giant networks. Factories have become part of global supply chains that spread the production of parts across different countries to make them better *and* cheaper. Banks have become part of global financial markets that trade trillions of dollars of mobile capital, and rely on international messaging platforms. Universities and scientists have built a web of collaborations across continents. Mass media, churches, sports bodies, criminal gangs and terrorists have all reorganized themselves to become part of massive networks that link up people and organizations across the planet.

And even states have come together in different sorts of networks. This includes global institutions governed by treaties, like the United Nations and the World Trade Organization; neighbourhood clubs, like the European Union or the African Union; and informal groupings, like the G7, the BRICS or the Organisation of Islamic Cooperation. What is more, there have been mushrooming links between intelligence agencies, courts, regulatory agencies, executives, and even legislatures that network with their counterparts abroad to tackle terrorism, organized crime, environmental degradation, money laundering, bank failure, and securities fraud.[10]

THE RULES OF NETWORKS

Networks have a number of features which make them unique.[11] Any network is only as strong as its weakest link – which is why we have seen so many disruptions to our global economy in recent years, with car manufacturing held up by shortages of semiconductors or Covid tests by a lack of specialist chemicals. But networks are constantly changing rather than static entities.[12] They are flexible and can reconfigure their components while retaining their goals if the environment changes. This is as true of reconfiguring your home music network as of your nervous system. Because they often don't have a single centre and can operate in a wide range of configurations, they can find ways of bouncing back from attacks. When one leader of al-Qaeda is captured another one can pop up. When a Japanese factory in China is closed by demonstrations, one in Vietnam can pick up the slack. And what's more, they are scalable – which means they can grow and shrink in size with little disruption. This is particularly true of the new networked companies that are springing up to take over the world.

They lead to contagion. Every child learns how a butterfly flapping its wings on one side of the world can cause a typhoon on the other. This is an inherent danger in connected systems: you get chain reactions. We have seen how epidemics and pandemics such as coronavirus, the plague, influenza, AIDS and foot and mouth disease gather pace until they become overwhelming. And when you add human reactions into the mix, these dynamics become even more complicated, leading some observers to talk about 'fearonomics'.[13] The fear of contagion, the flow of false information, and beggar-my-neighbour policies of individual states has accentuated the cost of financial, refugee and health crises.[14] The obverse of fearonomics is the speed at which a mood for political change can travel. Look at the case of Tarek el-Tayeb Mohamed Bouazizi, the Tunisian fruit-seller who set himself on fire in 2010 to protest about political corruption. Within two months, Tunisia's autocratic President Ben Ali had been toppled and the wave of protest soon spread to Egypt, where crowds gathered in Tahrir Square shouting: 'Tunisia is the solution.' Demonstrations also erupted in Algeria, Bahrain, Djibouti, Iran, Iraq, Jordan, Kuwait, Lebanon, Libya, Mauritania, Morocco, Oman, the Palestinian Territories, Saudi Arabia, Somalia, Sudan, Syria and Western Sahara. The form was almost as important as the content of these movements – they also inspired demonstrations against inequality (Occupy Wall Street), austerity (Los Indignados), even the price of cottage cheese (Israel).

The way that viruses, ideas and other entities spread reflects the structure of the network. We saw in Chapter Two how they encourage self-segregation into like-minded groups, or what scientists call homophily.[15] We have learned from games such as six degrees of separation that it is weak ties between different clusters that allow ideas or infections to spread across large distances. This is enhanced by a 'power law' that makes well-connected nodes become even more connected (allowing the rich to get richer, or making networks such as Facebook more useful with each new member they attract).[16] In fact, one of the most important qualities of a network is the effect of connection on all the nodes. That sounds fanciful – until you start to think about today's economy. As Tom Goodwin of the advertising agency Havas has pointed out, the world's largest taxi firm, Uber, owns no cars.[17] The world's most popular media company, Facebook, creates no content. The world's most valuable retailer, Alibaba, carries no stock. The world's largest accommodation provider, Airbnb, owns no property. For all of these platforms, their value comes from acting as an interface to the network. And being in a network changes the nature of all the nodes. An unused car can suddenly morph into a taxi, a spare room into a holiday destination (or a TV star into a president in the USA or Ukraine). The same is true of states when they are connected to new networks. As long as India and China were disconnected from the global economy, they were also peripheral to global politics. But their connection over the last thirty years has speeded up the creation of megacities, new industrial specializations and global supply chains, making these two giant civilizations much more politically influential.

One of the most interesting and under-researched features of networks is actually how they are also changing the nature of power.

THE CHESSBOARD AND THE WEB

The scholar and diplomat Anne-Marie Slaughter has argued that we need to update our mental maps of the world. Traditionally, leaders and diplomats saw global politics as a grand competition between states – a chessboard on which leaders play games of power politics. Slaughter concedes that this world will not disappear but offers a different model for global politics – as a web of networks where games are played not through bargaining but by building connections and relationships. She offers the arresting image of satellite photos of the world at night, with corridors of light marking roads, cars, houses, and offices. The lights stand for human relationships, where families and workers and travellers live and come together. 'It is,' she claims, 'a map not of separation, marking off boundaries of sovereign power, but of connection.'[18] Slaughter claims we need to develop a 'network mindset' to understand the dynamics of the non-hierarchical systems that define energy, trade, disease, crime, terrorism and human rights. In these areas, the chessboard's emphasis on states, sovereignty, coercion and self-interest are overshadowed by the web's orientation towards connections, relationships, sharing, and engagement.[19] It is the shift from a world of self-contained states to a huge web of entanglements that is changing the nature of global politics.

Early theorists thought that the rise of networks would lead to the decline of power politics. Networks connect people horizontally – allowing them to outwit old-fashioned hierarchies. They make it possible for the powerless to become powerful. The early stories of the internet age are filled with tales of Davids defeating Goliaths, plucky upstarts overthrowing or disrupting the establishment. The hope was that this would extend beyond the world of business to politics itself. In the wake of internet-inspired protests against the Iraq War, the former

Irish President Mary Robinson even called global public opinion the 'second superpower'. But the reality has been that so-called 'network effects' have created a winner-takes-all structure – allowing the rich to become ever richer and many of the most powerful to defeat the powerless. The internet is connecting people more than ever before, but not all connections are equal: power is becoming centralized in ever mightier hubs.[20]

In the business realm, Amazon, Facebook, Uber and Airbnb have helped to disrupt traditional hierarchies including retailers, newspapers, hotel chains, and taxi companies. They have empowered hundreds of millions of people, but at the same time they have concentrated enormous power in their platforms. The same has happened to politics, where single-party systems like the Chinese Communist Party and Putin's Kremlin have been strengthened rather than weakened by the internet. In connected systems, power is defined by both profound concentration and by massive distribution. Network theorists have found that similar dynamics govern all networks – whether they are studying proteins, neural networks, the financial system, social media or the economy.[21] There is a tendency to turn the world into cores and peripheries – the more power is spread to the periphery, the more powerful the core must become.[22]

If we go back to Anne-Marie Slaughter's framework, many globalists hoped that the web of connected countries would make the power games of chess players irrelevant. But it turns out that connectivity has not led to the end of competition. Globalization is not leading to a flat world, but rather a new topography of power. Some countries are more connected than others, and they can use these connections to enhance their power and prestige, and even turn them into weapons. Power politics has not disappeared – it has simply had to adapt to the asymmetries between cores and peripheries. The multilateral world of globalization has not displaced the multipolar world of great-power competition. The reality of twenty-first-century geopolitics is more about the fusion of the two. The network is the new board on which geopolitical games are being played out. Interdependence itself is being weaponized.

THE SEVEN HABITS OF HIGHLY EFFECTIVE CONNECTIVITY WARRIORS

In the last chapter we explored how all the connections that bind the world together – supply chains, trade routes, pipelines, railways, roads, cables, and the flows of people, goods, money and data – are becoming part of the currency of power. But the way that power is exercised depends on the topography of our networked world. The distribution of nodes, the density of ties and the emergence of dense hubs are creating a new map of power in the twenty-first century. All states are trying to control the high ground of this new world and identifying their strengths as well as the vulnerabilities of their opponents.

The terrains of power in this networked world – the mountains and valleys in each of the battlegrounds – create opportunities for different players to manipulate networks of finance, people, technology, and institutions. Once we start to look at the shape of each network we can understand the most efficient means of influence. In my research over the last few years, I have identified seven strategies used by the most effective states, the strongest connectivity warriors:

1. *Centrality.* The goal is to put yourself into a position where other people need you more than you need them. Then you can dictate the terms of the relationship. This is what Russia has tried to do with its energy markets, allowing it to blackmail countries like Ukraine or the Baltic states. People used to think that a relationship that benefits both parties would lead to harmony. But now states are

increasingly looking at the relative importance of the relationship to each side. They don't want to put themselves in a position where they are the needy party – and therefore open to pressure.

2. *Gatekeeping*. The the ability to decide who is 'in' and who is 'out' of the network. For example, the USA has effectively shut Iran out of the global financial system by threatening to exclude any banks from using the dollar if they trade with Tehran. Because 90 per cent of foreign exchanges involve the American currency, they have created a 'choke-point'. The European Union has also used the prospect of offering its neighbours membership of the club, or at least an association agreement with it, to transform their choices. Many countries are trying to make themselves into hubs in different sectors so that they can convert their position into influence, profit or power in a similar manner.

3. *Data-mining*. States tap into their control of a network to spy on others, something that Edward Snowden revealed was being practised by America's National Security Agency. If information flows through your cables or networks, you can end up with a treasure trove that can allow your country to get ahead and punish others.

4. *Subversion*. States get involved in other countries' systems and try to overturn the normal rules so that they no longer apply. Russia, for example, spreads disinformation about vaccines in the West, and about the financial interests of politicians in the post-Soviet space, in an attempt to spread chaos.

5. *Infiltration*. Rather than influencing a country from outside, it is often more efficient to change it from within. This might mean encouraging companies to invest, political parties to develop friendships or even citizens to emigrate. In recent times there has

been a controversial debate about the way that President Erdoğan appeals to Turkish minorities in European countries or Putin reaches out to ethnic Russians in Eastern Europe. Others talk about the role which Chinese settlers are playing in African countries and how their investments are helping skew the choices of local elites while changing the political orientation of many countries in which they have settled.[23]

6. *Rule-making*. The goal is to try to set the norms or rules for the whole network, just as the US did with domain names for internet sites and the European Union has done with its privacy regulations. Increasingly, the twenty-first century is turning into a battle to make the rules. China, a country that traditionally had to follow a rule-book set by others, is going to great lengths to define the regulations for new technologies such as 5G or artificial intelligence. It realizes this will give its national champions a commercial advantage. But more importantly, it can devise global rules that are compatible with its own interests and values.

7. *Independence-seeking*. If many powers are trying to weaponize their links with others, the best defence can be to minimize your dependence on them in order to free yourself from external manipulation. The USA has tried to do this with global energy markets, just as China is now doing with semiconductors and computer chips.

WINNERS, LOSERS AND THINKERS

Every connection between nations is part of a new map of power. A great power can become even greater by controlling its links to others. It can use regulations and set standards. It can manipulate financial or energy flows. It can restrict access to niche products or supply chains. It can build social media platforms or set search engine standards. It can even try to interfere with elections in other countries. Each power wants to take advantage of its unique position in the topography of our networked world to build spheres of influence.

But each power also brings a distinct philosophy and worldview, etched into its consciousness by the forces of history and geography. In that sense the twenty-first century will be as much defined by the clash of our ideas about connectivity as by the manipulation of the ties that bind us together.

For at least the next two decades, powers such as Turkey, Russia, Saudi Arabia, Iran or India will not be strong enough to set the global terms of competition. There are only three blocs armed with enough connections, money and institutional power to weaponize the whole system: the United States of America, China and the European Union. We're not far off George Orwell's dystopian vision of a world split between Oceania, Eurasia and Eastasia. It is to them that we will turn in the next chapter.

CHAPTER SEVEN:

EMPIRES OF CONNECTIVITY

The Pentagon is sometimes compared to a city within a city, but to a European accustomed to a smaller scale, it might seem more like a small country (the Department of Defense's 700,000 staff is bigger than the population of Luxembourg or Malta). Getting into the building is quite a hassle, with multiple document checks, each preceded by compulsory queues and airport-style security scans. But once you are in, you need never leave. The 600,000 square metre complex is filled with restaurants, supermarkets, gyms and shops for all seasons and occasions – from jewellery and chocolate to videos and pharmacies.

One person who seemed particularly reluctant to leave was the late Andrew Marshall, the founder and former head of the 'Office of Net Assessment'. First appointed to the role by Richard Nixon in 1973, every subsequent president confirmed him in the role, until he finally retired in 2015 at the age of ninety-four. Marshall was a legendary figure, known affectionately as Yoda within the defence community for his wisdom and creativity as well as his ability to spot and mentor talent. But while the original Yoda had the universally popular Luke Skywalker among his wards, Marshall's star protégés were rather more controversial, including former Vice President Dick Cheney and former Defense Secretary Donald Rumsfeld.

In his long career, Marshall's core speciality was always the future – analysing it and influencing it before others could catch up. He began his work as a nuclear strategist and in the 90s he commissioned a series of studies to define what he christened the 'Revolution in Military Affairs'. The RMA – as it became known – was about harnessing network technology to bring the battlefield into the information age with computers and precision-guided missiles.[1] Marshall was also one of the very first people to start seeing China as America's number one strategic threat – way back in the 1980s when the USA had embarked on a process of détente with a technologically backward and impoverished People's Republic. While successive administrations were working out how to reach out to China and turn it into a 'responsible stakeholder', Marshall's office spent its time organizing war games, studying Beijing's strategic thinking and ultimately planning for a potential conflict against China.

I went to see Mr Marshall in 2013 and was ushered in through a vaulted, steel-reinforced door to his Office of Net Assessment. When he walked in to greet me he was surprisingly spry for a man in his nineties. His only concession to his advanced years was wearing a fleece on top of his shirt and tie. He spoke slowly and was not afraid of silence, pausing after each point to let his ideas sink in.

What struck me the most in our meeting was how little he talked about weapons and technology – and how much he was worrying about the gap between Chinese and American ways of thinking. It is, in fact, no exaggeration to say that Marshall had become obsessed with the ways that the Chinese thought about our connected world. He told me that he encouraged policymakers in the Pentagon to read texts on 'eastern ways of thinking' such as the French philosopher François Jullien's

The Propensity of Things, The Geography of Thought by cognitive psychologist Richard Nisbett, and even books on Chinese medicine such as *The Web That Has No Weaver*.

He talked with fascination about an experiment by Richard Nisbett where Americans and Chinese were instructed to look at a fish tank. The Americans looked straight at the fish, following where they were swimming and how big they were. The Chinese, on the other hand, began with the shape of the tank, the stones and plants within it, and used their reading of the environment to understand what options were open to the fish. It is amazing, Marshall told me, to see the world through Chinese eyes. We in the West, he argued, are so focused on individual actions that we fail to look at the networks of connections that lie in the background. The Chinese, on the other hand, start by trying to understand the way these things shape the world and only see individual action as making a difference on the margins.

His Chinese opposite numbers would be flattered to hear of his interest: the fascination was mutual. In 2012, Major General Chen Zhou, the main author of four Chinese defence white papers, claimed that Marshall was the most important figure in changing Chinese defence thinking in the 1990s and 2000s: 'We studied the Revolution in Military Affairs exhaustively,' he claimed. 'Our great hero was Andy Marshall in the Pentagon. We translated every word he wrote.'[2]

I already could see, back in 2013, that these two countries were preparing for a new bipolar age. Both Marshall and Chen were products of the Cold War and their mental models came from a period of superpower confrontation. Their work was early preparation for what they saw as the next Cold War – splitting the world between China and America. And they fully expected that, as the world split back into two, the West which had been divided by the Iraq War and the financial crisis of 2008 would reunite. Europe would fall back into line as a junior partner in the free world.

But while the Americans and Chinese were examining their respective ways of understanding the power of technology – and its implications for world order – with mutual fascination, the Europeans set off in a different direction. Their foreign policy makers were not paying much attention either to Andrew Marshall or Major Zhou. The European Commission in Brussels had an alternative vision about its future relationship with China and America, and a completely different notion about the power of networks and their role in our future.

Influenced by the turbulent recent history of the continent, Europe had come to see networks as bridges between countries that allowed the world to avoid war, rather than weapons in a great-power confrontation. They thought of themselves as internationalists who wanted to build a strategic partnership with China alongside their alliance with the United States. It was obvious that even as the USA and China moved from a relationship of complementarity to one of greater competition, Europe would not neatly fit into the American camp. When I left Marshall's office, I was struck by the paradox that as we entered a period of total connectivity, the three major powers differed in the way they saw connectivity itself. And all around them is a fourth world of countries – including some the size of continents – that also want to plough their own furrows rather than play by someone else's rules.

Rather than a world split between authoritarianism and the free world, we will see the geopolitics of the twenty-first century play out as a battle between the three connectivity hyper-powers, and other states who navigate between them in a 'fourth world'. Each of these empires of connectivity has different weapons in its armoury. They also have very different philosophies. And each is currently going through a major process of evolution.

How do we reconcile the fact that great powers are becoming more similar with the fact that their different philosophies of connectivity are in conflict? The great powers are slowly coming together through the mimetic bind that I described earlier – but they are coming from very different places. As a result they are often, to borrow George Bernard Shaw's famous quip about America and England, 'divided by a common language': meaning quite different things when they use the same words. It is worth looking at each in turn, before seeing how our global order will be defined by the battle between these empires of connectivity. In the first chapter we looked at how the growing connections provided an opportunity for them to compete in new ways, how they were mirroring each other's techniques and how this was fuelling a connectivity security dilemma. In this chapter we can see how their emerging philosophies of connectivity relate to one another.

WASHINGTON: GATEKEEPER POWER

Traditionally American thinking about connectivity has been shaped by different tribes: the libertarian founders of the internet; the monopolistic entrepreneurs of Silicon Valley; the watchful eyes of the intelligence community; the Treasury's 'warriors in grey suits'; liberal internationalists in the State Department; as well as securocrats in the Pentagon like Andy Marshall.

These groups did not agree on everything but over time they settled on a modus operandi governed by some basic principles. They had universal ambitions and promoted a single and open internet which reconciled the idealism of the liberal internationalists, the expansive vision of the entrepreneurs and the power ambitions of the spies and geopolitical power-brokers. They also tended to be against heavy government regulation, whether because of their libertarian political instincts, their commercial goals or their fear of state capture by the likes of China and Russia. They would talk about supporting a liberal international order based on open societies, open governments, and an open international system. This philosophical approach follows squarely in the tradition of American liberal internationalism that bequeathed the world the Bretton Woods institutions, NATO and America's network of security alliances as well as its support for an 'open internet' and China's membership of the WTO. America's predilection for open markets and open societies resembled the UK's preferences during its hegemonic period in the nineteenth century. Because American companies enjoy pre-eminence in so many areas, openness was massively in their interest. And during the Cold War and post-Cold War periods, open societies used to be American allies – almost by default.

But even while talking about an open international system, Washington has systematically exploited its position at the heart of global networks to push forward two of the most effective tools we explored in the last chapter: gatekeeping and data-mining. The USA has used its privileged position as a hub to limit or threaten to penalize others. We saw in the last chapter that, after 9/11, officials in the US Treasury started exploring how Washington could leverage the ubiquity of the dollar and US dominance of the international financial system to target the financing of terrorism. By threatening to cut firms off from the dollar-based system they developed a stranglehold on the global banking sector. Even more dramatic is the way that the cover of the global war on terror allowed the USA to co-opt global communications networks as surveillance mechanisms.

But in 2016 America's attitude to connectivity changed dramatically. Watching an election that he did not participate in, Joseph Biden – along with other Democrats – saw how America's open society and neoliberal philosophy in its outlook towards the rest of the world had left it vulnerable to Russian electoral interference and Chinese economic coercion, which Donald Trump was able to exploit.[3] And that is why – even as they try to rejoin the world in dramatic ways – they are rethinking their approach to connectivity. While Biden talks about defending an open international order, he wants more protection for America from external interference. And he wants to have a more instrumental approach to global connectivity.

Team Biden rejects Trump's crude desire to put 'America First'. But Biden has claimed that his foreign policy will need to work for the middle class – and to protect them from the ravages of globalization.[4] The Democrats do not support a wholesale 'decoupling' of the American and Chinese economies – but they do want to make sure that trade talks keep jobs in the USA and defend America's middle classes rather than the profit margins of corporations.[5] This will involve developing a much stronger industrial policy which brings production for many key products back to the USA and its allies so that it is not open to being blackmailed by unfriendly countries like China (interestingly one of the very few papers the Biden campaign published before the election was on rethinking American supply chains).[6]

Biden's goal is to ramp up competition with China – but to do it in a way that avoids both a catastrophic hot war or the full decoupling of a cold war.[7] He does not contest Trump's notion that the Chinese were exploiting the open networked system against the USA – and that the US should respond in kind. But unlike the Republicans, he wants to do this by working closely with allies across Asia and Europe.

One of the drivers of this is a reassessment of US power. There was a big debate in the Trump administration too about whether the US had enough leverage alone to make China change its approach. The assessment of Team Biden is that the Trump experiment showed the limits of unilateralism. They think that only collective pressure and collective efforts to set rules will work in the longer term. The crux of their approach is a move from openness and integration with the whole world to a deeper integration and coordination only with trusted friends. For Biden's team this is seen as necessary rather than optional in the quest to preserve America's power and its technological edge. They have discovered that they will not be able to set global standards on 5G or semiconductors if they pursue a US-only approach.

Biden's team is also likely to be more open to the regulation of the digital sphere. Russia's interference in the 2016 presidential elections and the proliferation of fake news makes this inevitable. There are also geopolitical reasons for thinking again. One of the best ways of pushing back against Chinese expansionism and of recruiting allies in Europe will be to raise issues of privacy and regulation in the hope that China's big technology players – who are hand in glove with the Communist Party and Chinese state – will fail to meet the requisite standards of independence. It is probable that a Biden administration will subtly re-orientate the core strategies advanced during the Bush and Obama administrations to a more fragmented and multipolar world.

The Biden administration has signalled it wants to get back into the order-building business. However, this new 'system-building' is likely to be among a 'like-minded' group of democratic countries rather than through global institutions where China and Russia are veto players. This could lead to a greater fragmentation of the global system into rival friendship groupings.

BEIJING: RELATIONAL POWER

The China Foreign Affairs University was founded in 1955 by Mao's right-hand man, the then foreign minister Zhou Enlai, to train diplomats in Communist ideology and instruct them on how to promote permanent revolution around the world. It was forced to close during the Cultural Revolution but was reopened by Deng Xiaoping in 1990 to train a new generation of diplomats to reach out to the world, rather than transform it. I sometimes go to see the current president of the university, Qin Yaqing, when I travel to Beijing, drinking tea with him in the big formal armchairs of his meeting room or grabbing lunch in the restaurant across the road from his university. He is mild-mannered, with a smooth face and an unusually perfect grasp of English – reflecting his original training as an interpreter.

Qin is a serious thinker rather than a simple party hack. He first made his name in the Chinese academic community with highly regarded translations of the work of Alexander Wendt, one of the founders of a new(ish) school in Western international relations called 'constructivism'. He is much more dovish than most of the foreign policy intellectuals in China and is maybe less influential than some of the more hawkish voices (I have portrayed some of these licensed thinkers in my earlier books *What Does China Think?* and *China 3.0*).[8] But, in spite of his dovish nature and his detailed study of Western thinking – including as a foreign student at the University of Missouri-Columbia – Qin Yaqing is one of a small number of Chinese scholars who want to emancipate their country from Western thinking by developing a 'Chinese school of international relations' (something he has in common with Yan Xuetong, the hawkish academic we met in Chapter One). In his current role, Qin Yaqing is charged with training up the next generation of Chinese diplomats to sell Xi Jinping's China Dream to the world and to smooth the way for his ambitious Belt and Road Initiative.

Like Andrew Marshall, Qin Yaqing has studied Richard Nisbett's work *The Geography of Thought*. He was particularly struck by a passage which contrasts ancient Chinese with ancient Greek ways of thinking. The Greeks, according to Nisbett, thought of themselves primarily as independent. The core units of society are not groups but individuals. But the Chinese, on the other hand, saw themselves primarily as interdependent. The most important feature of their worldview is the relationship. Society, for them, is a collection of families bound by relationships of loyalty rather than individuals. While the Greeks saw the pursuit of liberty as the highest goal, for the Chinese – whether influenced by Taoism or Confucianism – the most important quest was harmony between these groups.[9]

Qin's thesis is backed up by Zheng Yongnian, a political scientist and informal government adviser who has studied how the internet and globalization have changed Chinese politics. 'The Western notion of the nation state is as a legal society,' he said to me in an interview in early 2021, 'but China is a "relationship society".' In practical terms he thinks this starts with the different circles of the family radiating out from the father. Zheng says that this hierarchical model also extends to the political system. Just look at the architecture of the Beijing ring roads, he says. The centre is the Communist Party HQ on the first ring. Then you have the government on the second ring road. The National People's Congress is on the third ring. The people's consultative committee is on the fourth ring and so on.

Professors Qin and Zheng argue that this Confucian focus on relationships also shapes how China sees our interconnected world – and contrast this with Western perspectives. Zheng argues that Westerners tend to see international relations in terms of geography. But for China, what matters is not the geographical distance between two countries but how close they are socially or politically. 'If the political distance is close I will give it more [favourable treatment],' he says, 'and put it in a very close ring to me. If I feel it is further I will put it in the third or fourth ring.' He uses the example of China and Australia, who share a geography but argue a lot – 'not because of national interests but because they don't feel they are close to us politically'.

Professor Qin says that the Confucian system also gives the Chinese a different idea of power. Westerners, he argues, see the individual state as the key to international relations. They measure power by comparing the technology, military, economy and institutions of each state. The Chinese, on the other hand, are less focused on the individual states themselves and more on the nature of their relationships to others (although Chinese think-tanks do exhaustively map the 'comprehensive national power' of different countries). The most powerful countries are the ones with the most links to other states, and those most central to the system. For Confucians the way you should treat other actors in the world depends on how much loyalty they show to you. Rather than trying to convert others to your values and your way of life, you should attempt to find ways of mutual coexistence.[10] The Confucian system depends on the exchange of favours (*renqing* – 人情) and punishments rather than on the rule of law.[11] It is this Confucian system that bound Koreans, Japanese and Mongols into tributary relationships with a dominant China during the Ming dynasty (AD 1368–1644).

Many see it as the model inspiring the Chinese President Xi Jinping as he seeks to develop the Belt and Road Initiative, a practical vision for recreating the *Tianxia* (天下), a community of common destiny centred around China. Xi Jinping thinks a lot about his role in history. And this is leading to a big rethink about how China deals with globalization and its dark side. In 2020 Xi Jinping launched a new vision under the slogan of the 'dual circulation economy'.[12] Zheng Yongnian was one of nine hand-picked scholars invited to a symposium with the Chinese president to discuss the idea, held in August 2020 in the Communist Party headquarters in Zhongnanhai.

Behind the technical-sounding phrase lies an idea that could change the global economic order. Instead of operating as a single economy that is linked to the world through trade and investment, China is fashioning itself into a bifurcated economy. One realm ('external circulation') will remain in contact with the rest of the world, but it will gradually be overshadowed by another one ('internal circulation') that will cultivate domestic demand, capital, and ideas. The purpose of dual circulation is to make China more self-reliant. After previously basing China's development on export-led growth, policymakers are trying to diversify the country's supply chains so that it can access technology and know-how without being bullied by the United States in some of the ways we examined in Chapter One. In doing so, China will also seek to make other countries more dependent on it, thereby converting its external economic links into global political power.

As part of this rethinking of economic links Xi Jinping has expounded the concept of 'big security' (*da an* – 大安). Rather than just worrying about invading armies and navies, China now needs to protect itself from the dangers of interdependence being manipulated in almost every area of national life, from financial ties and trade to telecoms and newspapers.[13] His mission is to reduce China's exposure to globalization. Zheng Yongnian explained the significance of this: 'Everything can become a security issue because the two countries are too interdependent. China will put more energy in its own technology development. Some degree of decoupling is inevitable and good for the relationship.' Some of the most eye-catching initiatives are 'Made in China 2025' and 'China Standards 2035', which are designed to allow the country to become 70 per cent self-sufficient in the most important technologies of the future. Xi Jinping has also tried to reduce China's dependence on the dollar by diversifying Chinese investments and experimenting with a digital renminbi (RMB) as well as a new payment system that avoids connections with the US currency.

In the summer of 2020 the Chinese authorities approached some of the biggest foreign companies in China, asking them to prepare to send a senior representative for a top secret, small, closed-door meeting on China's new economic strategy with a senior official at an undisclosed time and location. As so often in China, the form of the event echoed its content. According to two people with direct knowledge of the matter who insisted on anonymity to discuss it with me, the organizers asked companies to send only ethnically Chinese representatives, a perfect metaphor for a vision that sees Beijing trying increasingly to develop its own technologies, its own energy sources and to rely on its own consumption rather than relying on foreigners. Under dual circulation, Beijing's new rules on data, research and development, and standards will force prominent Western companies to acquire Chinese characteristics, unless they withdraw from China altogether. As one well-placed private-sector observer put it to me, 'China's idea is that if companies like Daimler or Volkswagen want to work in China, they will have to move services, R&D, and new products there. Beijing hopes that dual circulation will transform them into Chinese companies.'

Xi Jinping's approach is extreme but it echoes the philosophy of previous Communist leaders – from Deng Xiaoping onwards – who wanted to balance the economic opportunity of opening up to the West with the risk of its opening China up to regime change or blackmail. These considerations led to the cautious process of opening and reform being married with policies such as capital controls, the Great Firewall and moves to promote indigenous innovation.

As well as taking defensive action to stop foreigners changing China, Xi Jinping also sees interdependence as a potential source of leverage over other countries due to their own vulnerabilities.[14] The Chinese government and scholars are carefully studying the American debate on 'decoupling' and are exploring how to respond in kind. When China was less powerful it spent a lot of time thinking about how to overcome its weakness to challenge the USA through America's networks. The most detailed agenda for an aggressive approach to connectivity came in a book called *Unrestricted Warfare*, which shot into the Chinese bestseller lists in 2001. The book sets out a series of strategies for 'non-military warfare', arguing that 'soldiers do not have the monopoly on war' (see Table One overleaf).

Xi Jinping is looking at how to weaponize connectivity from a position of strength rather than weakness. He is using China's huge domestic market to bully other countries into following Beijing's lead.

His officials have threatened to withhold medical supplies, close markets and withdraw investments from countries that do not comply with China's demands. And Xi Jinping certainly seems to be following ancient Chinese thought in the implementation of the Belt and Road Initiative. His master plan seems to be underpinned by a desire to turn China into the central power in the world – the Middle Kingdom! The Belt and Road is based around linking China with the rest of the world – and showing goodwill to countries that show sufficient deference to Beijing. It involves flexible relationships which are not overly constrained by rules or institutions. Even though China's trade and economic power are leading to ever-growing links with the rest of the world, its most innovative geo-economic tool has been infrastructure, physical, virtual and institutional. China today is using connectivity more frequently, more assertively, and in a more diverse fashion than ever before.

TABLE ONE: The many facets of unrestricted warfare

MILITARY	TRANS-MILITARY	NON-MILITARY
Atomic warfare	Diplomatic warfare	Financial warfare
Conventional warfare	Network warfare	Trade warfare
Bio-chemical warfare	Intelligence warfare	Resources warfare
Ecological warfare	Psychological warfare	Economic aid warfare
Space warfare	Tactical warfare	Regulatory warfare
Electronic warfare	Smuggling warfare	Sanction warfare
Guerrilla warfare	Drug warfare	Media warfare
Terrorist warfare	Virtual warfare	Ideological warfare
	(deterrence)	

Source: Qiao Liang and Wang Xiangsui, *Unrestricted Warfare* (Beijing: PLA Literature and Arts Publishing House, 1999)

BRUSSELS: RULE-MAKER

You may not have heard of Margrethe Vestager but she has been hailed as a saviour of the connected world. As the European Union's Competition Commissioner, she is one of the few with the power and confidence to take on the digital giants that have produced our networked world, companies that have grown larger than many countries. Over the last few years, she has fined Google €8.2 billion for including Chrome on its Android browser and trying to shut other players out of online advertising. She fined Apple a record €13 billion for tax avoidance (plus a further €1.2 billion in interest). She went on to introduce a new digital rulebook – clunkily named the General Directive on Privacy Regulation (GDPR) – which forced companies to obtain explicit consent from consumers before gathering and monetizing their data. In 2019, Vestager set her sights on Facebook and promised to investigate its new digital currency, Diem (formally known as Libra).[15]

Not everyone agrees with the detail of each policy – in fact the European Court of Justice recently overturned her landmark decision to fine Apple – but it is hard not to be impressed by her audacity. Most governments treat the digital revolution like the weather – something you need to adapt to – but her ambition is nothing less than to control the seasons.

Vestager is a unique figure. She managed to catapult herself into one of the most powerful jobs in the world in spite of coming from one of the smallest parties in one of Europe's smallest countries (she was the inspiration for the prime minister in the acclaimed Danish TV show *Borgen*). She is the internet's supreme tech regulator but she refuses to use Google, whose privacy policies she disapproves of (she opts for the European DuckDuckGo instead). She is a believer in the potential of the technological revolution, but she wants politics to shape it. She is known as a pragmatist, but she is also a stubborn defender of moral rectitude. Vestager's ethics are no doubt influenced by her upbringing by two Lutheran pastors. But though Vestager's biography is unique, her attitude to networks and rules is not. The Vestager agenda is, in fact, a perfect expression of the European Union's attitude to connectivity.

The European Union has done as much as any other power to promote the emergence of a networked world. Although European politicians often evoke the mirage of a country called Europe – complete with flag, anthem, currency, and passports – the EU is no super-state. It is a decentralized network which allows countries to have the best of both worlds – a continent-sized market and currency but tailored politics at a national level. The EU's different centres of power, or 'nodes', are member states, European institutions and other actors, which share power horizontally, rather than vertically according to the rigidly pre-defined blueprint of a constitution. They are all interdependent, and though they carry different weight on different issues, no node, however powerful, can afford to ignore the others. An open network system like the EU wouldn't survive for very long if it were purely about instrumental cooperation – its founders recognized the need to have clear rules and norms that govern what everyone is allowed to do.

This is one of the paradoxes the EU faces. On the one hand it agrees passionately with Adam Smith that trade and interdependence tame nationalism and militarism. But, at the same time, once you break down the barriers between yourself and others, you need to make sure that they do not abuse their access. So the more openness you have to others, the more common rules you need. When new countries want to join the EU, they need to integrate over 80,000 pages of law – governing everything from gay rights and the death penalty to lawnmower sound emissions and food safety – into domestic legislation. This is the EU's operating system, otherwise known as the '*acquis communautaire*'.

The EU does not just abide by this operating system itself – it has

tried to make anyone else who comes into contact with its network follow the same rules. This export of regulations has been extended into
the EU's dealings with outsiders and there are values clauses in every
single trade deal and association agreement it signs. Because the EU has
the world's largest single market, even multinational companies depend
on access to the region.[16] Europe uses this economic power to put forward its idea of how society should be organized – threatening to
exclude companies that do not live up to its norms.

For example, in its competition with China, Brussels is not just trying
to get access to the China market, it is trying to defend Europe's social
model which includes higher wages and social protection. In environmental and food protection, Europe is much more risk averse than other
powers. It has adopted a 'precautionary principle' of assuming the worst
will happen and trying to pre-empt the problem, rather than clearing up
the mess afterwards. This is the philosophy that lies behind the EU's ban
on genetically modified organisms (GMOs) and its prohibition of
chlorinated chicken and beef with hormones, which has put it at loggerheads with the United States. The EU also has norms that protect
cultural diversity and the role of agriculture in the stewardship of the
countryside. The so-called 'Brussels effect' has made the EU the world's
standard-setter in many areas, including computer software, children's
toys, cosmetics, household appliances and food safety.[17]

Margrethe Vestager has been following a pattern of behaviour set by
her predecessors, but she has drawn extra attention because she started
to use these powers on an industrial scale. When I spoke to Peter Thiel
in California, he confided to me that many tech companies in Silicon
Valley fear Brussels more than Washington. 'They understand Washington and know how to influence it,' he explained, 'but they don't
understand how to influence the EU although they fear that bad things
will come from there.'

Vestager's ability to impose European preferences on the rest of the world stems from the EU's unusual structure and its dominant role in global trade. But this imposition is only possible because it adheres to them within the club. This kind of regulatory power is less costly, more durable, more deployable, and less easily undermined by competitors than more traditional foreign policy tools. We should not forget that the European goal in promoting global networks was not, first and foremost, to develop a new instrument of power. It has always been part of a vision of a world that transcends power politics. Europeans have rejected the idea of realpolitik and military power as a way of solving disputes – trying to move towards a situation where disputes are resolved through the courts. They believe in the civilizing power of trade as a means of avoiding war. And though they believe in market economies, they do not believe in market societies and are trying to protect their social models, cultures and environment from market forces. Above all they hope that the networked world can be governed by an 'operating system' that values 'shared sovereignty' over national sovereignty.[18]

THE FOURTH WORLD

Most of the world's population do not live in the USA, China or the European Union. And many are acutely aware of the ambivalent effects of connectivity. On the one hand, many states have benefited from it. They have seen their economies surge as a result of globalization and the opportunity of being tied into the supply chains of the three great economic motors: the USA, China and the European Union. The price of raw materials – from oil and gas to copper and aluminium and cobalt and lithium – has risen rapidly. New inflows of investment have become available. And some citizens have had the chance to follow their dreams with migration. At the same time, many of the same countries remember from colonial times the exploitation, loss of control and humiliation of being turned into the periphery of someone else's empire. Their big fear today is once again having to follow diktats from the three big empires of connectivity – and being forced to choose between them rather than being sovereign over their own destiny.

That being said, the new world provides medium-sized powers with more options in geopolitics than in the conventional twentieth-century balance of power, where they were outclassed by the superior technology and firepower of the superpowers. This has led to various niche strategies.

Russia has turned itself into a pioneer of societal disruption. Its recent foreign policy – including gas outages, sanctions, worker expulsions, cyber attacks, disinformation campaigns and efforts to gridlock Western-led international organizations from the UN to the Organization for Security and Co-operation in Europe (OSCE) – has successfully shaped the behaviour of its neighbours and other powers. In an age of mass migration, Turkey has used its ability to control flows of people into Europe as a source of power, demanding the lifting of visa restrictions and financial aid to mitigate the burden of hosting more than 3 million Syrians. Even with low oil prices, Saudi Arabia leverages the 10 million barrels of oil it extracts every day, accepting short-term losses in order to shape global markets to its advantage (and to the disadvantage of rivals such as Iran, Russia or US shale companies). What's more, it has been willing to invest billions of petro-dollars in support of its foreign policy goals – supporting counter-revolutionary regimes such as that of Egypt's General Sisi during the Arab uprisings, and waging a proxy war against Iran in Yemen. Conscious of the expiry date on its oil advantage, Saudi Arabia is now trying to lead the way to a post-carbon future and cement its role long-term as the leading economic power in the Middle East. Iran mirrors Saudi ambitions in its links to the Shia communities spread across the region, coupled with its support for militias such as Hamas, Hezbollah and the Houthis, which wage wars on its behalf. It has also been willing to disrupt global energy markets by attacking ships in the Strait of Hormuz, and by launching cyber and drone attacks on the Saudi oil giant Aramco to disable its facilities.

As we head into the middle of the century, there will be at least as many Africans as there are Indians or Chinese. Africa is the next frontier of emerging markets, which is why – after decades of being a geopolitical afterthought – every great power is now trying to deepen its engagement with the continent. Europeans and Chinese are battling to sign up African countries to their respective standards on data privacy; while the USA has become more interested in the continent as a way of countering China's rise to global prominence. But although many of these African countries are set to become important players, the fifty-four nations of Africa are so divided politically that they're unlikely to be able to exercise collective power at the global level in the foreseeable future. What is more, very few Africans would agree with the idea that the age of globalization has broken down borders. Even wealthy Africans with prestigious jobs complain that getting visas to come to Fortress Europe or the United States has become humiliating, and is indeed driving Africa to engage ever more with China. For those less fortunate it is precisely the impossibility of moving legally that creates the threat of large migrant flows, as they risk their lives to come over illegally (and then stay in their countries of arrival) rather than moving back and forth in a regulated way. The Western perception that this has been the age of movement shows how invisible these realities have been to policy-makers.

In the Pacific Rim, we can see how Japan, Korea, Australia and ASEAN all try to maintain economic ties with China while hedging militarily with the United States of America. Many of these countries have been pioneers in recalibrating their interdependence and cutting China out of the most sensitive parts of their infrastructure such as 5G, in order to prevent the Chinese from capturing their data. They have also been actively trying to work together and forge much closer relationships with powers outside their neighbourhood in order to increase their freedom of action.

The most important open question in the fourth world is probably India, an ancient civilization with vast ambitions for the modern era. It has the potential to become a pole of its own, but its attitude so far has been defensive rather than strategic. It is also no surprise that, after its traumatic history of imperialism, the debate about 'data colonialism' is most lively in India. Delhi's technological prowess in key sectors and its huge market could make it an important player in setting the norms for our technological future. And its diaspora of 20 million gives it a reach into every other country in the world. India's decision in 2020 to ban over two hundred Chinese apps from Indian networks and to restrict Chinese investments in Indian companies sent shockwaves through the Chinese system, as India is the only market with the potential to become as big as those of the USA, EU and China itself.[19] If China can sell its technology products in India, it can still benefit from huge consumer markets, even if excluded from the West.

There is an active debate now within India about whether to follow China in shutting out foreign suppliers and aim for autonomy and localization. But so far there has been much less focus on developing a 'Hindu philosophy of connectivity' that could rival the international reach of the USA, China and Europe. Instead the debates about connectivity have tended to be more defensive. It is only a decade since the Indian government began to rethink its ban on building roads and railways up to its border with China. After the war between the two Asian giants in 1962 there was a fear that transport links might be used by Chinese troops to make incursions into Indian territory (a fear that was revived in 2020 with some violent border clashes that saw twenty soldiers killed and dozens injured). At the same time there is much concern that the Chinese Belt and Road Initiative will allow Beijing to 'encircle'

India and rewire its neighbourhood in ways that are inimical to Indian interests.

TABLE TWO: One planet, three visions of connectivity

	EU	CHINA	USA
PHILOSOPHY	Normative	Relational	Instrumental
STRATEGIES	Gatekeeper (membership) and rule-making	Centrality (centrality to the system and benefits)	Gatekeeper (choke-point) and data-mining (surveillance)
POWER INDICATOR	Wellbeing of EU consumers and companies	Number of ties and centrality	Capacity (GDP, military, tech)
CURRENCY	Rules	Relationships	Resources
PRECAUTIONARY PRINCIPLES	Banning GMOs	Pre-crime arrests	Preventive war

Instead of moving into a bipolar world or the ungovernable chaos of a non-polar one, what we are seeing emerge is a 'four-world order'. Three empires of connectivity have fundamentally different ideas about how to organize the planet, while the remaining countries – amounting to a fourth world – are forced to navigate between them.

The USA is increasingly decoupling from China and using its centrality in the system to export its foreign policy preferences. One of the key aspects of the US policy of China containment is the idea of the Economic Prosperity Network: in short, rebuilding a separate world for 'like-minded' democratic and market economies to trade, invest, transfer data and produce value chains under their own rules. Because the USA has lost faith in the prospect of bringing China back towards market (or democratic) convergence, it wants to rebuild a parallel universe from which Beijing is excluded.

The American rethink is being encouraged by Beijing's 'Made in China 2025' policy and its Belt and Road Initiative. These policies are designed to catch up with American development and bypass the USA by building links with the rest of the world. China used to seek access to Western-centric networks while preserving its sovereignty. But today, its main goal is building new networks with itself at the centre.

At the same time, the European Union is still trying to defend universal institutions like the WTO, IMF and World Bank, but increasingly having to act on its own behalf as these become gridlocked by great-power competition. The EU is also moving from a situation where it had a near-religious attachment to promoting interdependence in a globalizing world towards one where it is more interested in asserting its own sovereignty in a more contested world order.

Superficially the 'fourth world' is in a similar predicament to the 'Non-Aligned Movement' during the Cold War, but its prospects are more promising. The 'four-world order' is characterized by high levels of contact between the different blocs – not just through the formal institutions but in the intense economic exchange between different countries. Where many of the so-called 'non-aligned' countries found themselves stranded during the Cold War, today they will try to take advantage of benefits from all three orders, although all of the powers will attempt to make them pick a side.

The key terrains of this new world include all the battlegrounds described in Chapter Five: the economy, infrastructure, technology, migration, and international law. Our three great powers have developed a new armoury of weapons and defences. In the place of tanks and planes they now use regulation and standards, transit control, supply chains, propaganda, sanctions, encryption, monetary policy and financial systems. But it is not just their interests that divide them; they look at the connected world through different eyes.

When Washington looks out at the world it sees hubs in the network map – exploring where it can use them for surveillance or sanctions. When Beijing looks at the world, it looks at the ties – exploring how it can connect other countries to its market and use these infrastructure links to bind them into a Chinese sphere of influence. And when Brussels looks at the world it looks at the individual nodes – or more specifically the welfare of European consumers and companies – and thinks about what norms or rules will best serve their interests.

Even when they use the same language they can mean different things. Take the idea of the precautionary principle. In Chinese hands, this often means using artificial intelligence to spot suspicious behaviour by individuals and arresting them *before* they commit a crime. In America, it often means 'preventive strikes' with drones against terrorists who threaten American security. And in Europe it might mean abolishing genetically modified organisms.

Looking forward, some of the biggest dangers will come when these different systems clash in the 'four-world order'. Xi Jinping is not the only leader who has developed a notion of 'big security' for the interdependent age – the USA and Europe have as well. And these 'big' concepts of security are leading the jurisdiction of these players to impinge on other great powers. For example, the USA has been using the global reach of the dollar to impose its Iran policies on other players by introducing 'secondary sanctions' on companies that continue to trade with the Islamic Republic. This forced big European companies like Total and Airbus to withdraw from billion-euro contracts with Tehran – even though the European governments in the countries where they are domiciled were keen for these deals to proceed. The European equivalent has been imposing its rules on data privacy and competition policy on American and Russian companies by making their access to European markets conditional on living up to EU norms. The Chinese example has been to try to silence opponents of its policies around the world, by threatening to withdraw access to its market. Within China, there is an unspoken deal that companies and citizens can get on with their lives and prosper, as long as they avoid getting involved in politics. Now this deal is being exported to the rest of the world as China threatens foreign governments, sports teams, universities, fashion houses and film production companies with sanctions if they speak out over China's policies on Hong Kong, Xinjiang, Taiwan, Tibet or the management of Covid-19.

The continuing presence of these three universalist projects signifies that there will be a lot of conflict in future years. In fact, we could see new flashpoints around connectivity in some of the very places that divided the world in previous eras.

One front-line state that has returned in a new form is Belgium, where I spent most of my childhood. The small, flat country has always been the canary in the coal mine of global conflict – from the Napoleonic period to the Second World War, foreign troops have always marched through Belgium when they clashed with each other. And the same is happening today – but today's conflicts are about global regulations rather than trench warfare. One which we examined earlier was around SWIFT, a financial information service that gives banks access to global financial markets. When the United States took aim at the Iranian economy, one of its first ports of call was to put pressure on SWIFT to cut Iran out of its system. The board of the Belgian-registered company complied – raising enormous questions about European sovereignty. Brussels will continue to be a central front for many other types of regulation – between China, America, and Russia – as well as a player in the future.

Another battleground for connectivity is the Balkans, the combustible region that spawned the First World War. This is where the old empires meet – Russia, China, Turkey, Europe – in a battle for hearts and minds. But the new conflicts between these players are very different from those that divided the great powers a century ago. These days, the EU is competing with Russia and China over access to energy pipelines, rules for getting government contracts and the regulation of their economies.

If the Balkans were the tinder box of the early twentieth century, the Indo-Pacific will likely be the equivalent for the first half of the twenty-first century. Thinkers like Yan Xuetong have warned of a war over Taiwan or some of the atolls and islands in the East and South China Seas. But we could also see competition over small states like Vanuatu, Papua New Guinea or Tonga. What is at stake is not the *Lebensraum* of earlier eras but control over trade routes and connectivity in the globalized world of the twenty-first century.

There is also a new scramble for Africa. In the nineteenth century, all the European empires competed with each other to claim land and resources. And today there is a new frenzy of activity among the great powers to increase their engagement here. The goal today is not only to plunder natural resources, but to tap into the fastest growing economies and markets. From 2010 to 2016 more than 320 embassies were opened in Africa.[20] The contest was not just between Europe, China and America but Saudi Arabia, Russia, India and Turkey too. Each of these powers is hoping to sign Africans up to its own rules and standards in battles over data and internet regulation, naval bases, trade routes, and measures to regulate the flow of people.

In future years the big flashpoints in geopolitics are less likely to be about control of the land and the sea. Instead they will be about migration pacts, offshore financial centres, fake news factories, state aid, computer chips, investment protection, and currency wars. As well as fighting to access the flows of our connected world, the 'four-world order' will increasingly become a contest to write the rules governing connectivity itself.

DISARMING CONNECTIVITY:
A MANIFESTO

When many Americans imagine the future of geopolitics they think of Hawaii. If you sit in the office of the Indo-Pacific Commander in Camp H. M. Smith on the island of Oahu and look out at the Pacific Ocean you feel a bit like Captain Kirk on the deck of the USS *Enterprise* in *Star Trek*, in the last outpost defending liberal international order from the chaos beyond.

Hawaii's role in the American psyche is well known. It was here that America was born as an imperial power when its navy used military force to bring about regime change in 1893. It was also here – with the attack on Pearl Harbor – that America stepped up as a global power in the twentieth century. More recently it was here that Barack Obama came of age intellectually and embraced the idea of a different model of American leadership, one that included a 'pivot' or 'rebalancing' towards Asia. And it is at Camp H. M. Smith that a military nerve-centre is preparing for the possibility of a war with China.

What is less well known is that Hawaii was the 'cradle of the Chinese revolution'. Sun Yat-sen, the founder of modern China, was a pupil at Punahou school in the Hawaiian capital, the same elite school that Obama attended as a child. 'This is my Hawaii,' Sun Yat-sen told the newspaperman Albert Pierce Taylor in 1910. 'Here I was brought up and educated; and it was here that I came to know what modern civilized governments are like and what they mean.'[1] Sun Yat-sen – who founded the Revive China Society (興中會) in Hawaii in 1894 – developed some of the vision and the slogans that have been used by Xi Jinping in his early talk of the 'China Dream' and the 'revitalization of the Chinese nation'.

Many of the dreamscapes of today's geopolitics first took shape amid the palm trees, sunsets and dramatic shorelines of this isolated archipelago. Positioned exactly between North America and Asia, it is on these remote islands that the American and Chinese dreams were forged in the nineteenth century, that the convergence of the two superpowers continued in the twentieth century, and that a military conflict is being prepared in the twenty-first century. It shows that the world is not big enough for two grand visions about how to organize the planet (not to mention the less militaristic third one being developed in Europe) – and that if they are not somehow insulated from one another they will collide.

But in my mind, the real lesson of Hawaii for our world has less to do with the control of the seas than with the ambivalent nature of our world. The structure of the Hawaiian economy speaks volumes about the double bind of globalization. Half of the state's GDP comes directly from the US Department of Defense, who see the islands as the front line in their battle with China. The other half comes from tourism, in particular from weddings, which attracted over 100,000 visitors to the islands and $16 billion of spending in 2018. Hawaii's economy is literally powered by love and war. Hawaii's condition – of being torn between connection and conflict – is becoming a paradigm for the world. But while the two sides of Hawaii's economy are largely separate, harmony and discord in the wider world are more intimately linked. Our planet is experiencing both the best and the worst of times because of one single phenomenon: connectivity.

THERAPY FOR THE AGE OF UNPEACE

When I started working on this book I originally intended to make a passionate plea for an 'open world'. As I said in the introduction, I hoped to design a new architecture for a more united planet. But the deeper I delved, the more I became aware that the good and bad features of connectivity are inextricably entwined – and that it is impossible to untangle them without destroying many of the biggest advances in our civilization.

On the one hand the ties that bind our globalized world have made it better than ever before. Wars and extreme poverty are receding. Life expectancy has surged. Billions are receiving an education. And the big challenges of the twenty-first century – from pandemics and climate change to financial crises and mass migration – will only be solved by working together. But at the same time, our connections are leading to a tribalization of the world, with populist leaders promoting national glory over global understanding. As competing superpowers instrumentalize the climate and our health, humanity may be brought to the brink of extinction. And behind the headlines a pandemic of connectivity attacks is ripping through the world, heralding a dangerous age of unpeace.

People crave control and autonomy, but they are far from ready to give up on the convenience of the internet, not to mention global travel and trade. As a result, international politics has become more and more like a dysfunctional relationship, in which the partners aren't able to split up but can't stand being together either. Globalization has given many nations untold wealth and convenience, but it has also given them the opportunity, the motive and new weapons for conflict.

I had an epiphany about the dilemma facing our world during one of my trips to Beijing. While browsing in my favourite bookshop, the Book Worm, I came across a volume called *Facing Codependence* by Pia Mellody, which seemed to capture all the pathologies that beset contemporary politics and international relations. Rather than talking about relationships as a balanced phenomenon, it identified a condition called 'codependence', during which the ties between different players become toxic, but also inescapable.

Sufferers struggle to set functional boundaries between themselves and others. They have problems managing interdependence. They oscillate between delusions of grandeur and feelings of inferiority. The only surprise for me was that I had found this diagnosis of our age of unpeace in the self-help section of the bookshop, rather than the politics section.

On the surface, Mellody's book sounds like classic American psychobabble but I became convinced that the codependency analogy could be helpful in managing world politics. For one, her diagnosis of our condition is not rooted in the pathology of individual people or countries but in the nature of the relationships between them. It recognizes that tensions stem as much from psychology as economics. They are intrinsic to the global system we have created and can be managed and channelled, but not eliminated. Maybe most importantly, she starts with the lived reality of her patients rather than the theories of experts – and tries to find a way of making the patient feel safe rather than telling them that they are mistaken in their fears. Reading Mellody in Beijing I also came to see that while the notion that problems need to be managed rather than fixed is unsettling for children of the Western enlightenment, it is more familiar to Asians, whose dominant philosophies tend to present the world as more open-ended, with yin and yang coexisting rather than being synthesized.

That is when I realized that the world needs therapists rather than architects. Rather than eradicating connectivity's dark side with a grand design, we need strategies for shaping and surviving our new reality. In the Cold War people realized that the biggest threat to humanity was that the nuclear arms race could spiral out of control – and they tried to use the escalation to build trust and gradually bring the weapons that threatened to wipe out humanity under control. Our own dilemma is much greater because in the age of unpeace all the violence flies under the radar of war, and is therefore unregulated. And rather than being trapped in a few deadly technologies that can be counted, surveyed and controlled, we are living through an era where almost anything can be weaponized.

If the connections that are essential to our wellbeing are also being turned into deadly weapons, we need to find ways of making them less dangerous. For all these reasons I have become convinced that rather than ending connectivity, we should try to devise rules and norms that take the sting out of it or disarm it. If the Cold War was eased by arms control, the equivalent for our age is 'disarming connectivity'. This will be a Sisyphean struggle that resembles the ongoing therapy required to detoxify personal relationships. Although psychologists do not think you can ever fully cure codependency they have laid out five steps to manage it so their patients can still lead a fulfilled life.[2] I have tried to adapt these treatments into a five-step programme for the age of unpeace, based around the idea of 'disarming connectivity'.

Step One: Face up to the problem

The first step in all therapy programmes is facing the problem. At the root of our global tensions are the grievances of individuals, whose lives have been made insecure, stressful and unpredictable by our connected age. Social media exacerbate fragmentation and unleash envy and resentment. Rather than telling people they are irrational or wrong, politicians must express a deeper understanding of people's lived experience. The starting point must be to change the way we gather data. Rather than the abstract and aggregated statistics of 'Esperanto economics', we need to find a way of measuring wellbeing that reflects different lived experiences. This will mean having much more localized data that explore the relative performance of different groups.

Going back to my Brexit example in Chapter Three, one can see how the aggregated data on the overall effect of freedom of movement hid many of the specific and local negative effects. For example, surveys show that wages went down significantly in some sectors like construction after freedom of movement was introduced, while there was pressure on public services in neighbourhoods that had attracted a lot of inward migration.[3] Having these data – and using them to understand different segments of the population – will help governments communicate in a way that connects while developing policies that can really help those who lose out from connectivity. It is important to measure economic questions against fears about loss of status, and the dilution of the rules our societies live by, or the identities people hold.

Since the backlash began, many governments have been trying to rethink globalization – to parse different types of interdependence into the good and the bad. The good parts are the ones which allow the world to benefit from economies of scale, provide solutions to problems that cut across borders and promote peace by agreeing limits on violence and weapons of mass destruction. Added to that are the cultural riches of free travel, expanding horizons and better food. On the other hand, the dark side of globalization includes free-riding, changes to identities, unfair competition, and malicious actions. All the great powers seek to navigate a path between unconstrained global connectivity and national protectionism. In America they talk about 'decoupling' from China. In Beijing, they are championing the 'dual circulation economy'. And in Europe, the quest is for 'strategic autonomy'. These three concepts all hint at the same insight – that connectivity can be dangerous as well as beneficial.

Step Two: Establish healthy boundaries

I talked in the introduction about how all the things that are meant to bring us together seem to be driving us apart. Paradoxically, the best way to unite the world is to create enough distance to make people feel safe and in control. The dividing line should be between 'managed' and 'unmanaged' togetherness, rather than 'open' and 'closed' societies.

For example, a group of Chinese and American economists and lawyers have sought to find a middle ground between what they call 'deep integration' and 'decoupling' for US–China trade.[4] Individual nations must have the freedom ('policy space') to design the policies that best fit their preferences – even if they are misguided and counter-productive! They begin with respect for sovereignty, they draw red lines around 'beggar-my-neighbour' policies and suggest some negotiated ways of resolving differences.

Others have sought to reconcile global mobility with national identity. In 2000 the Dutch politician and intellectual Paul Scheffer published an article in which he claimed that the Dutch multicultural integration model had failed. 'We are living in the Netherlands alongside each other but without ever meeting one another,' he declared. 'Each has his own café, his own school, his own idols, his own music, his own faith, his own butcher, and soon his own street and neighbourhood.'[5] In a thoughtful book, some years later, he laid out a different approach to integration.[6] In exchange for being allowed to move to the Netherlands, newcomers would need to sign up to specific norms designed to safeguard Dutch liberalism. Increasingly, politics will need to show that it honours the culture and history of the majority population even as it protects the rights of minorities (incidentally, usually through legislation that protects the rights of the majority as well).

The political scientist Jonathan Haidt has suggested some ways of navigating the polarized landscape around ethics and culture which has had such a crippling effect on American national political life. He claims that the best way of honouring the culture of others is to begin by stressing what a society holds in common rather than its diversity, as a way of opening up a new political space.[7] And, in the realm of technology, we have seen academics, psychologists, legislators and even tech companies themselves trying to explore how the internet can lead to social integration – and how to avoid it descending into the toxic territory of 'social snacking' and 'social comparison'.[8] The British House of Lords has even raised the idea of a 'Magna Carta for Artificial Intelligence' that would not only protect the privacy of individuals but also ensure that human intelligence maintains control over the ethical questions involved in the use of machines.[9]

Politics has to offer greater protection to the losers from economic openness, finding ways of specifically catering for the 'left behind'. It may seem like a minor policy but, in Denmark, the Social Democrats reformed the pensions system to allow people who began work younger – often without going to university – to get their pensions earlier. What was unique about this measure is that it was a reform which specifically helped people who had not gone to university – the group that feels most exposed to the ravages of global competition. In all these areas, the goal should be to introduce healthy borders to allow contact but reduce the risks of connectivity, so that citizens stop feeling the need for the protection of walls. Interdependence can only survive in the long term if it feels safe once again.

Step Three: Be realistic about what you can control

Hoping for a convergence around a centrist globalist philosophy seems utopian and counter-productive. The alternative approach – of seeing competition as a 'systemic rivalry' that our side must win at all costs – could be equally dangerous. If we see all points of contact between countries as sites for 'systemic rivalry' we will be doomed to live with permanent insecurity. The continuing presence of three universalist projects – in the USA, China and EU – signifies that there will be a lot of conflict in future years.

In the 1990s and early noughties many Americans and Europeans hoped to convert China, Russia and other powers to Western liberal democratic ways of working and thinking. But people are now coming to terms with the fact that China will not collapse and it will not become like the USA either. The solution therefore is to work out how to live with a powerful China, while remaining true to our own values. Rather than pinning our hopes on conversion, the goal is now to insulate Western economies and political systems from Chinese interference. This is leading to an idea of 'selective decoupling', for example opening yourself up to buy Chinese steel but staying away from communications infrastructure like 5G.

Rather than coming up with a new architecture or philosophy to rewire global politics, the best we can do right now is to recognize the dangers inherent in connectivity and try to manage them. Sigmund Freud once wrote to one of his patients that her therapy would be a success if it could turn her 'hysterical misery into common unhappiness'. The equivalent for international politics would be to transform uncontrolled connectivity conflicts into a tough competition, with limits and rules to mitigate the risks.

In order to make connectivity safe, states need to establish recognized boundaries to their own behaviour, similar to the ones they created after the invention of the aeroplane and the atomic bomb. In other words, humankind has to learn to govern the technology it has created. At the moment the system allows for unlimited escalation. This needs to give way to rules for survival. World order could be built like a Russian doll. The outer layer – with a very small number of rules designed to prevent the destruction of the planet through war or the climate crisis – would apply to all countries. Within that global container, smaller dolls could develop more extensive rules. For example, democratic countries might choose to develop norms on the regulation of data or new technologies. And within the democratic world, different regional organizations such as the European Union can develop much thicker rule-books among their own members. The goal should be to develop laws as closely aligned as possible to the citizens who have to live with them.

Step Four: Self-care

Our experience over the last fifty years is that equal, free, prosperous states tend to be better neighbours and more constructive international citizens than those that struggle with authoritarianism, extreme inequality or political chaos. While it is right to recognize the vulnerabilities of Western democracies to manipulation by states such as Russia or China, I think the biggest challenge to the liberal order comes from within our divided societies. And that is where we need to focus the bulk of our attention. The generational challenge for internationalist leaders is to redesign their national education, healthcare, social care, welfare and industrial policies to produce wealth and distribute it fairly at home. Building domestic strength and self-confidence is the strongest foundation for international engagement.

Earlier in this section, I described some of the political compromises that will be needed to reach out to those who feel they have lost out from global connectivity, which will be a necessary precondition for preserving an open order on economics, politics and migration. There will be trade-offs between the need to preserve domestic consent and the need to organize our affairs effectively on the global stage.

For example, many people argued earlier in the century that the United States and Europe should develop a new Transatlantic Trade and

Investment Partnership (TTIP) as part of their quest to set the rules for the twenty-first century. The economic benefits that this project promised were limited, but the political adjustments that would be needed to get such a deal through were very visible. Soon, grassroots campaigns sprang up against TTIP in Germany (where citizens feared having to eat chlorinated chicken) and in the UK (where people feared that the National Health Service would be forced to accept competition from private healthcare companies based in America). As a result, a project designed to forge a new generation of transatlantic harmony in the twenty-first century ended up fuelling fear and mutual suspicion. There are important lessons in this episode for leaders in democratic countries who want to operate at a transcontinental scale in order to influence China.

Step Five: Seeking real consent

The big difference between the age of unpeace and the Cold War is the fact that it involves ordinary people. It is true that people in Hawaii and other places used to have to do 'duck and cover exercises' to prepare for nuclear Armageddon. But most of the action took place a long way from their everyday lives – and they certainly were not invited to the arms control talks in Reykjavik. By contrast, violence in our age of unpeace plays out in the smartphone in our pocket rather than the jungles of Vietnam or deserts of Afghanistan. And so we too need to be involved in working out how to implement a disarmament agenda.

We know from human relationships that there is a single principle that is key to any kind of legitimacy: consent. And that is the one thing which has been most conspicuously lacking when it comes to connectivity. Governments and companies, from free-trade deals to Facebook, have driven forward connectivity without any serious attempt to secure consent either domestically or internationally. Most countries (democratic and non-democratic alike) felt that they had very little choice in

accepting the whole economic, political and values package. Domestically people felt they didn't have the chance to say 'no' or even 'slow
down', given the depth of political consensus behind the agenda; while
some global companies operated in almost completely uninhibited
fashion. Indeed, politicians and businesses even framed what they were
doing as part of a benign mission, to which there was also no real alternative. Of course you could theoretically opt out of everything by being
North Korea or refusing to use modern communications but, for most,
it was essentially an all-or-nothing choice. The results of this non-
consensual connectivity have then been various forms of resistance or
outright revolt.

An alternative agenda would be characterized by working hard to get
real consent for contact between peoples and nations. That means tech
companies that are subject to real democratic control; countries whose
polities want accelerated trade and free movement pressing forward
even faster while others choose to opt out, and an overall framework
that makes those choices possible and discreet, so that people don't feel
they have to overturn the whole of society to have their voice heard or
to stop the specific thing they don't like.

Of course this approach poses a bigger question: whose consent?
And how should it be sought? To take Britain and the EU as a starting
point: British membership of the EU was based on explicit consent by
Parliament and the public in a referendum. The counter-argument from
Brexit supporters is that the public did consent to a more limited version of Europe but not everything that followed. And it is true that there
was never a real engagement in building support for the level of migration that free movement entailed after enlargement of the Union. The
argument was just that it was a net economic benefit and people should
live with it. Equally, today, there has been no serious attempt to engage
with the 48 per cent who voted to remain and who feel equally bereft
and disenfranchised. Rather than trying to secure consent from those

who value more connectivity with Europe, there's just an almost gleeful stripping away of their (our) rights. It's another version of maximalism and majoritarianism without rooted democratic consent, this time in the abrogation of connectivity. There is a real question about how to achieve consent in conditions of polarization. Our elected institutions are creaking. And referendums don't seem to do any better at healing divided societies. But from Iceland to Estonia people are trying out new forms of deliberative politics, while leaders in countries such as Denmark seem to be able to reach across the divide between classes and ethnicities. Rather than giving up, it seems like an urgent question for our generation to take on.

AN INTERVENTION

This book explains the many ways in which globalization – and in particular the digital revolution – make conflict more likely. We are already getting hints of the future as our unified global economy starts to be driven apart with skirmishes over access to vaccines, rising prices due to delays in supply chains, spiralling disinformation campaigns, the widespread use of sanctions, the politicization of refugee flows, and arguments about climate change protectionism. Unchecked by our actions, the logical conclusion of these trends would be a dystopian world of mass inequality where the politics of envy leads to ever more violent and aggressive policies, and the ties that bind us together provide ever more powerful weapons through which this conflict is to be fought.

If we continue on our current trajectory of greater connectivity, greater comparison and greater competition, we risk entering an age of perpetual conflict, not officially at war but never at peace, in which no one can remember the origins of our disagreements. As the technologies of destruction become ever more powerful, the stakes in this forever conflict will continue to rise until they risk taking the world over the edge.

Although we're only at the beginning of this phase in human history, the hidden conflicts of interdependence already hurt more people than war – but they could become much more dangerous still. The nightmare scenario is a layering of explicit attacks that fall short of war coupled with the manipulation of global challenges. You might see catastrophic cyber attacks, financial crises and an economic depression triggered by a collapse of global supply chains. These could be reinforced by a failure to tackle the climate crisis, which could in turn provoke a migration crisis and further pandemics.

The realities of Covid-19 and climate change have made it easy to conjure up apocalyptic scenarios, but our leaders and our fellow citizens have struggled to adapt their behaviour to avoid them. If they fail, the costs of unpeace could be a descent into the sort of destruction that has begun to fade from living memory in much of the world.

But I am not a fatalist. Just because trends have established themselves over the last few years does not mean that our downfall is inevitable. Human history is not predetermined. Politics has the power to change course. And what's more, with recent changes in America and Europe, it already has. Covid has begun to sketch out the beginning of a framework for cooperation on future pandemics (although the West and China have not yet really joined forces). We are developing a more subtle debate about how to manage the technology that has enabled us to develop vaccines, feed the world, store renewable energy and connect the world. The huge recovery plans in Europe and America – coupled with the political awakening I have just described – should allow both continents to build back better. They have already taken some of the steps I laid out in my therapy for a connected world by working to establish healthy boundaries, self-care and seeking greater consent from their people.

At times of major change, it is more glamorous to point the way to a new Jerusalem or sketch out the architecture for new world order. But I am convinced that the therapy being sought in Washington and European capitals will be better. It does not offer any permanent solutions to the challenges of unpeace, but it does promise a chance to avoid its worst side effects. By introducing the right therapy into our politics now, we can lay the foundations for a major reset. And in the long run the architecture could be different too.

We have started a new quest to preserve some of the advances of interdependence without stumbling into catastrophe. It involves recognizing that connectivity, whether we like it or not, is a double-edged sword. Once we accept that it means conflict as well as cooperation, we can benefit from the strategies that minimize discontent and limit the violence it brings in its wake. As with all psychological maladies, the first step back to health is to acknowledge that there's a problem. That is the ultimate purpose of this book. It is an intervention.

ACKNOWLEDGEMENTS

It takes a network to understand a networked world. And this book is a product of collective intelligence as much as individual scholarship.

Five extraordinary institutions have inspired and supported my study of the interconnected world.

This book first came to life in the breath-taking beauty of Villa Serbelloni, the Rockefeller Foundation's retreat in Bellagio, on the banks of Lake Como. I will forever be grateful to an anonymous benefactor who nominated me for a fellowship which I took up in the aftermath of the Brexit vote. I learned so much from the other fellows with whom I shared meals, Aperol spritz, and the surreal experience of witnessing Donald Trump's election in the bedroom which JFK had used when he visited the villa. Over the course of four weeks I worked through my political grief, living on a monastic timetable with a daily rise at 4 a.m. and work till 6 p.m., stopping only for breakfast, lunch and a run around the grounds of the villa. My cohort of fellows expanded my horizons with expertise from psychology, network science, epidemiology, anthropology, and stories of the colonial experience and its aftermath. I am grateful to Claudia Juech for having initially invited me, to Pilar Palacia for hosting us with such compassion and to Rockefeller's president Rajiv Shah and his colleague Matthew Bishop for inviting me back in 2019 for a joyous 'Bellagio 60 Homecoming' reunion where I reconnected with other fellows as well as being inspired by Rockefeller's remarkable network of change-makers.

My writing started at a cracking pace but when I returned to work reality set in and my progress stalled until I was invited to take up a second fellowship in late 2019 at the Institute for Human Sciences in Vienna. Under the leadership of Shalini Randeria and Ivan Vejvoda the Institute took extraordinary care of my temporal as well as my spiritual needs, accommodating me in a beautiful apartment in Vienna's Jewish district and affording me a peaceful daily walk across snowy Vienna to have lunch at the Institute. While there I enjoyed many fascinating conversations with other fellows such as Misha Glenny and Claus Offe, as well as the joy of seeing Ivan Krastev, Dessy Gavrilova and their wonderful children.

A third institution I am indebted to is the World Economic Forum (WEF) for giving me so many insights into many of the trends I describe. They appointed me chairman of the 'Global Agenda Council on Geoeconomics' from 2015 to 2017. I learned so much from that experience from colleagues such as Karan Bhatia, Ian Bremmer, Parag Khanna, Hina Rabbani Khar, Paul Laudicina, Michael Levi, Kishore Mahbubani, Moises Naim, Doug Rediker and Dmitri Trenin. I am grateful to Klaus Schwab for honouring me as one of the WEF's 'Young Global Leaders' and bringing me to Davos many times to understand the big trends in the world, as well as to Borge Brende for being such a great partner and teacher of geopolitics in his roles at the forum and as Norwegian foreign minister.

The ambition, bravery and creativity of the Open Society Foundations have been a constant inspiration. I have learned more from the ideas and example of George Soros than I can ever express in words. One of the great joys of recent years has been having the chance to work with his son Alex Soros, who is increasingly shaping the foundations' activities with his own passion, intelligence and ideas. Mark Malloch Brown, a mentor and friend, is one of the most inspiring architects of global political change. He has been uniquely able to move mountains in national politics, international bureaucracy, boardrooms and global civil society. Leonard Benardo continues to amaze me with his intellectual range, his cultural omnivorousness, and his kindness. Laura Silber has been a good friend, always willing to give shrewd counsel and advice. Maria Cattaui, Michael Ignatieff, Anatole Kaletsky, Daniel Sachs and Anya Schiffrin on the global board have all been intellectual allies in rethinking global politics.

Most importantly I need to thank the remarkable people involved in the European Council on Foreign Relations (ECFR), the organization I have the privilege to work for. I want to thank Mabel van Oranje, my partner in founding it, and our extraordinary board members Carl Bildt, Franziska Brantner, Ian Clarkson, Marta Dassu, Lykke Friis, Teresa Gouveia, Sylvie Kaufmann, Ivan Krastev, Adrzej Olechowski, Norbert Roettgen, Javier Solana, Marietje Schaake, Alex Stubb and Helle Thorning-Schmidt, who have inspired me, supported me and taught me so much about our connected world. My colleagues have also been true intellectual soulmates. Alba Lamberti and Vessela Tcherneva, my friends and fellow leaders, have been the most wonderful partners through the craziest of times. Jeremy Shapiro, Anthony Dworkin, Andrew Small, Janka Oertel, Jana Puglierin and Vessela Tcherneva have all patiently helped me puzzle through many of the thorny topics addressed in this book, reading fragments, proposals and chapters and helping to make them better. At ECFR I have had the joy of working with three extraordinary research assistants who have become the closest collaborators and partners: Ulrike Franke was working with me at the start of this enterprise in 2016, and first helped conceptualize the ideas on the weaponization of interdependence that I initially explored in an edited volume on 'connectivity wars'. She was followed by Jonathan Hackenbroich in 2017, who encouraged me to persevere, brainstorming so many of the big ideas with me in front of many whiteboards. He has taken on some of these themes in his own pioneering work on economic coercion. Most recently Lucie Haupenthal, a remarkable thinker, organizer and collaborator, has been a daily partner on Zoom and Teams and the telephone, although the lockdowns have stopped us from meeting in real life. I have also benefited hugely from exchanging ideas with my brainy colleagues Asli Aydintasbas, Julien Barnes-Dacey, Susanne Baumann, Piotr Buras, Susi Dennison, Ellie Geranmayeh, Swantje Green, Gustav Gressel, Alexia Gouttebroze, Adam Harrison, Carla Hobbs, Joanna Hosa, Anna Kuchenbecker, Andrew Lebovich, Kadri Liik, Hugh Lovatt, Tarek Megerisi, Theo Murphy, Folke Pfister, Nicu Popescu, Chris Ragett, Ana Ramic, Jose Ignacio Torreblanca, Tara Varma, Artuo Varvelli, Nick Witney, Andrew Wilson, Denica Yotova and Pawel Zerka. Jennie Bradley and Roxanne Ford, my executive assistants, have allowed me to criss-cross the planet, kept me sharp and organized, and brightened my days with their kindness, resourcefulness and good humour. Finally, I benefited from a talented group of interns who have undertaken research tasks during the five summers I have worked on this book: Johann van der Ven, Archie Hall, Ravi Veriah Jacques, Yasmin Samrai, Xiaoran Hu, Abel Ribbink, Joshua Peterson, Hanna-Sofi Bollman and Valeriia Barannikova.

Apart from my colleagues, a number of other people provided generous and penetrating comments on a series of drafts, helping me refine the argument:

Joseph Nye, whose own work on complex interdependence laid so many of the foundations for my book, has been a friend and supporter for many years. He helped tease out some of the big topics in several phone and video calls and generously commented on the very first draft.

Anthony Giddens, the university teacher who did the most to shape my worldview as an undergraduate, then reshaped it once again in adult life by persuading me to study how the digital revolution is changing everything, and by co-curating a series of ECFR workshops studying its effect on globalization, politics, economics and human nature.

Andy Moravcsik helped me to see the flaws in an early draft with a tough but justified critique, while Anne-Marie Slaughter gave me renewed faith in the enterprise at the end of the process with some brilliant comments and pointers on the structure of the book. Her own pioneering work on the grand strategy of our connected world continues to inspire.

Olaf Corry took time to read a very early draft, giving me brilliant feedback and helping me understand our planetary dilemmas around climate change. George Lawson applied his unique blend of IR theory, sociology and history to my narrative about the global order. Parag Khanna, who continues to amaze me with his energy and ambition, has been working on many of these themes for years and gave me brilliant guidance at a critical moment. Hans Kundnani helped me more than he will realize, with his sceptical response to a very early draft.

The most dramatic testing ground for my ideas is the emerging competition between America and China. Jeremy Shapiro has been a great partner in trying to understand the USA as well as so much else in our interconnected world. Janka Oertel and Andrew Small have been the greatest partners in understanding both the grandest arc and the minutest twists and turns in this historic relationship from the Chinese side. I also benefited from comments from Agatha Kratz, Zhang Feng and the omniscient Kevin Rudd, who can integrate grand strategy with an intimate knowledge of both China and the USA. It was Joshua Ramo who first inspired my interest in China decades ago. He kindly read this draft and reminded me once again what a great friend and intellectual companion he is. He has taught me so much about technology, global politics and the art of living.

There are two people who have been the closest intellectual supporters of my intellectual awakening while writing this book:

Adam Lury, whose orthogonal brain never ceases to inspire me, has consistently encouraged me to seek fresh angles for understanding our world. It is amazing to think that his own novels on pandemics and data were written two decades ago.

Ivan Krastev has been an intellectual godfather and the most generous of friends, reading numerous drafts and offering me sanctuary on the Bulgarian coast and in Vienna when I needed to escape from the Brexit madness or the relentlessness of organizational life.

Ivan also encouraged me to sign up with Toby Mundy at Aevitas Creative Management, one of my happiest decisions. I have admired Toby's engagement with ideas for over two decades and feel privileged to relaunch my writing career under his shrewd, creative and thoughtful representation. Toby in turn introduced me to Alex Christofi, a brilliant editor at Penguin Random House, who suggested the title for the book and whose subtle interventions have embellished its every page. It has been a joy to be edited by someone who is such an accomplished writer in his own right.

During the process of writing I have been sustained by some of my oldest friends. Kate Bradley, Lucie Emerson, Joanna Fell, Shauna McAllister and Siobhan McInerney-Lankford have been in my life since I was an obnoxious child in Brussels. Jamie Coulthard, Helen Parr and Toby Green have helped keep me sane since Cambridge. I am also grateful to friends I made at the Foreign Policy Centre over two decades ago. Sunder Katwala has taught me so much about the politics of identity and helped me make the book comprehensible to non-foreign policy types. Rob Blackhurst provided advice on how to bring the ideas to a wider audience. Richard Gowan offered wisdom on lawfare and global governance. And Phoebe and Richard Clay, together with their intrepid children, have shared wonderful food, conversation, wild swims and campfires with my family in Selsey, Warwickshire and London, holding us accountable every year to the resolutions we rashly made the year before.

When the tsunami of Brexit–Trump–Covid-19 struck, my family was my anchor and my guiding light. I happily traded my vagabond existence for the chance to be with them every single day. It is to them that this book is dedicated.

I owe everything to my parents, who have lived through the toughest of times with courage and love. My father Dick Leonard, who died at the age of ninety on 24 June 2021, awed us daily with his resilience, integrity and productivity. His example inspired me to persevere with the book. My mother, Irene Heidelberger-Leonard, packs more intelligence and compassion into a single day than most people manage in a lifetime. She not only sustained my father through a series of health emergencies but has been the most extraordinary grandmother, matriarch and intellectual force. The loyalty and companionship they shared in daily calls with Berni and Annele and John and Marjorie is moving. And the kindness and medical brilliance of my cousins Richard and Andrew have literally kept us alive – as well as sane – during the coronavirus. I want to cry every time I think of it.

Miriam and Phiroze have touched me with empathy, friendship and intellectual companionship that knows no bounds. It has been a joy to see the blossoming friendship between their precocious son Isaac and his cousins.

My children, Jakob and Noa, have given me daily joy and support during the toughest moments of writing. I will never forget how Jakob, as a kind and clever seven-year-old, made me a poster on 24 June 2016 making the case for Britain to rejoin the EU ('don't worry Daddy we will bring Britain back when we are older'). Four years later his sister Noa, at the age of eight, took it upon herself to design a wonderful cover for this very book, in the process demonstrating her unmatched intellectual prowess, artistic skills and capacity for love. Now that the writing of the book is over I Iook forward to spending even more of my weekends and early mornings with these extraordinary human beings.

Finally, I must thank my wife Gabrielle Calver. You have been my best friend for twenty-five years and so many parts of me now bear your beautiful imprint. Our enforced confinement during the lockdown has been a precious gift, impressing on me even more vividly how much I love you and how much I need you. We would all have fallen apart without your generosity, creativity and spirit of adventure. In the words of Bob Dylan, 'If not for you . . .'.

ENDNOTES

INTRODUCTION: THE CONNECTIVITY CONUNDRUM

1 Keith Bradsher and Ana Swanson, 'The U.S. Needs China's Masks, as Acrimony Grows', *New York Times*, 23 March 2020, <https://www.nytimes.com/2020/03/23/business/coronavirus-china-masks.html> [accessed 10 November 2020].

2 The insight that connectivity and conflict are connected is not new, but as old as Jean-Jacques Rousseau and more recently Karl Polanyi. Robert Keohane and Joseph Nye in the 1970s pointed out in *Power and Interdependence* that asymmetrical interdependence is an important source of power. Scholars such as Dani Rodrik, Fareed Zakaria, John Ruggie and Jürgen Habermas, Dan Drezner, to name just a few of many, have argued that one of the great issues of our times is how to limit economic, military, cultural and social interdependence in ways that preserve its benefits while protecting people against dislocation to an extent that satisfies populations. I first wrote about the 'weaponization of interdependence' in my essay collection on connectivity wars in 2016 (Mark Leonard (ed.), *Connectivity Wars: Why migration, finance, and trade are the geoeconomic battlegrounds of the future* (London: European Council on Foreign Relations (ECFR), 2016). These topics have been explored in academic circles further by Henry Farrell and Abraham L. Newman in a widely cited article on 'weaponized interdependence' published in *International Security*, 2019.

3 Leonard (ed.), *Connectivity Wars*.

4 Ibid.

5 Yuval Noah Harari, *Homo Deus: A Brief History of Tomorrow* (New York: Harper Collins, 2018).

6 Fergus Hanson and others, 'Hacking democracies', Australian Strategic Policy

Institute, 15 May 2019, <https://www.aspi.org.au/report/hacking-democracies> [accessed 25 October 2020].

7   According to the Uppsala Conflict dataset, there were 1,183,079 fatalities in state-based armed conflicts, non-state conflicts or due to one-sided violence between 2001 and 2019. 'Uppsala Conflict Data Program', Department of Peace and Conflict Research, <https://ucdp.uu.se/exploratory> [accessed 16 December 2020].

8   Lucas Kello, *The Virtual Weapon and International Order* (Yale University Press, 2017).

9   Mark Leonard, *Why Europe Will Run the 21st Century* (London: 4th Estate, 2005).

10 Mark Leonard, *What Does China Think?* (London: 4th Estate, 2008).

11 European Council on Foreign Relations, www.ecfr.eu.

12 International Relations realists have long recognized that interdependence can bring conflict as well as cooperation, e.g. Kenneth N. Waltz, *Theory of International Politics* (Boston, MA: McGraw-Hill, 1979).

13 Parag Khanna, *Connectography: Mapping the Future of Global Civilization* (New York: Random House, 2016).

14 Steve Morgan, 'Top 5 Cybersecurity Facts, Figures, Predictions, And Statistics For 2021 To 2025', *Cybercrime Magazine*, 8 January 2021, <https://cybersecurityventures.com/top-5-cybersecurity-facts-figures-predictions-and-statistics-for-2021-to-2025/> [accessed 10 February 2021].

15 John Thornhill, 'Time to save the internet', *Financial Times*, 14 January 2021, <https://www.ft.com/content/4e27089f-5a99-4fa4-8713-9420f5e5a611> [accessed 10 February 2021].

16 Anthony Giddens, Foreword to Carla Hobbs (ed.), *Europe's digital sovereignty: From rulemaker to superpower in the age of US-China rivalry*, ECFR, 30 July 2020, <https://www.ecfr.eu/publications/summary/europe_digital_sovereignty_rulemaker_super-power_age_us_china_rivalry> [accessed 5 October 2020].

17 'The new political divide', *Economist*, 30 July 2016, Leaders section, <https://www.economist.com/leaders/2016/07/30/the-new-political-divide> [accessed 10 October 2020].

CHAPTER ONE: THE GREAT CONVERGENCE

1   'Xi addresses World Peace Forum', *China Daily USA*, 7 July 2012, <http://usa.chinadaily.com.cn/2012-07/07/content_15557706.htm> [accessed 10 October 2020].

2   Niall Ferguson and Moritz Schulatrick, 'Chimerical? Think Again', *Wall Street Journal*, Opinions section, 5 February 2007, <https://www.wsj.com/articles/SB117063838651997830> [accessed 25 July 2020].

3 Joseph Nye, 'Power and Interdependence with China', *Washington Quarterly*, 43, no. 1 (2020), 7–21, <https://www.tandfonline.com/doi/full/10.1080/0163660X.2020. 1734303>; Julian Gewirtz, 'Chinese Reassessment of Interdependence', *China Leadership Monitor*, no. 64 (2020); Kevin Rudd, 'To Decouple or not to Decouple', University of San Diego, Robert F. Ellsworth Memorial Lecture, 4 November 2019.

4 Nye, 'Power and Interdependence with China'.

5 Nye, 'Power and Interdependence with China'; 'World Development Indicators', World Bank, <https://databank.worldbank.org/reports.aspx?source=world-development-indicators#> [accessed 3 November 2020].

6 Alyssa Leng and Roland Rajah, 'Chart of the Week: Global Trade through a US–China Lens', *Interpreter* (Lowy Institute), 18 December 2019, <https://www.lowyinstitute.org/the-interpreter/chart-week-global-trade-through-us-china-lens> [accessed 2 July 2020].

7 C. K. Tan and James Hand-Cukierman, 'Face recognition trailblazer SenseTime rushes to be next Google', *Financial Times*, 18 August 2019.

8 Ibid.

9 'The Talent', MacroPolo: Decoding China's Economic Arrival, <https://macropolo. org/digital-projects/chinai/the-talent/> [accessed 2 July 2020].

10 Bernard Marr, 'Meet the World's Most Valuable AI Startup: China's SenseTime', *Forbes*, 17 June 2019.

11 Tan and Hand-Cukierman, 'Face recognition trailblazer SenseTime rushes to be next Google'.

12 'SenseTime "Smart AI Epidemic Prevention Solution" Helps Control Coronavirus Cross-Infection', SenseTime, 14 February 2020, <https://www.sensetime.com/me-en/ news-detail/23783?categoryId=21072> [accessed 2 July 2020].

13 Josh Horwitz, 'The Billion-dollar, Alibaba-backed AI company that's quietly watching people in China', *QWuartz*, 16 April 2018.

14 'SenseTime, the Chinese AI giant blacklisted by Trump, sees demand surge during coronavirus', *Bloomberg*, 19 August 2020.

15 Tan and Hand-Cukierman, 'Face recognition trailblazer SenseTime rushes to be next Google'.

16 Kai Strittmatter, *We've Been Harmonised: Life in China's Surveillance State* (Exeter: Old Street Publishing, 2019).

17 Ibid.

18 Ibid., p. 174.

19 Zou Shuo, 'Chinese students studying abroad up 8.83%', *China Daily*, 28 March 2019, <http://www.chinadaily.com.cn/a/201903/28/WS5c9c355da3104842260b30eb.html> [accessed 2 July 2020].

20 Bethany Allen-Ebrahiman, 'The Man who Nailed Jello to the Wall', *Foreign Policy*, 29 June 2016.

21 Strittmatter, *We've Been Harmonised*, p. 173.

22 Paul Mozur, 'One Month, 500,000 Face Scans: How China is Using AI to Profile a Minority', *New York Times*, 14 April 2019.

23 Kenneth Roth and Maya Wang, 'Data Leviathan: China's Burgeoning Surveillance State', *New York Review of Books*, 16 August 2019.

24 Christian Shepherd, 'China's SenseTime sells out of Xinjiang joint venture', *Financial Times*, 15 April 2019.

25 Roth and Wang, 'Data Leviathan: China's Burgeoning Surveillance State'; Mohd Ayan, 'China's forced sterilisation on the Uyghur women: a gross violation of human rights', LSE blog, 13 October 2020, <https://blogs.lse.ac.uk/socialpolicy/2020/10/13/chinas-forced-sterilisation-on-the-uyghur-women-a-gross-violation-of-human-rights/> [accessed 2 December 2020].

26 Siminia Mistreanu, 'Life Inside China's Social Credit Laboratory', *Foreign Policy*, 3 April 2018, <https://foreignpolicy.com/2018/04/03/life-inside-chinas-social-credit-laboratory/> [accessed 2 December 2020]; Nicole Kobie, 'The complicated truth about China's social credit system', *Wired*, 7 June 2019, <https://www.wired.co.uk/article/china-social-credit-system-explained> [accessed 2 December 2020]; Strittmatter, *We've Been Harmonised*.

27 Sherisse Pham, 'The United States Strikes a Blow to China's AI Ambitions', *CNN Business*, 10 October 2019.

28 Rebecca Fanin, 'Facebook Copies China's WeChat Once Again. Who Would Have Guessed This?', *Forbes*, 20 June 2019.

29 Shoshana Zuboff, *The Age of Surveillance Capitalism: The Fight for a Human Future at the New Frontier of Power* (New York: Public Affairs, 2019).

30 Guy Rosen, 'New EU Report Finds Progress Fighting Hate Speech', Facebook, 23 June 2020, <https://about.fb.com/news/2020/06/progress-fighting-hate-speech/> [accessed 2 July 2020].

31 Ryan Browne, 'Edward Snowden says "the most powerful institutions in society have become the least accountable"', CNBC, 4 November 2019, <https://www.cnbc.com/2019/11/04/edward-snowden-warns-about-data-collection-surveillance-at-web-summit.html> [accessed 10 July 2020].

32 Barton Gellman, 'NSA infiltrates links to Yahoo, Google data centers worldwide, Snowden

documents say', *Washington Post*, 30 October 2013, <https://www.washingtonpost.com/world/national-security/nsa-infiltrates-links-to-yahoo-google-data-centers-worldwide-snowden-documents-say/2013/10/30/e51d661e-4166-11e3-8b74-d89d714ca4dd_story.html> [accessed 15 July 2020].

33 Glenn Greenwald, 'XKeyscore: NSA tool collects "nearly everything a user does on the internet"', *Guardian*, 21 July 2013, <https://www.theguardian.com/world/2013/jul/31/nsa-top-secret-program-online-data> [accessed 16 July 2020].

34 David Cole, '"No Place to Hide" by Glenn Greenwald, on the NSA's sweeping efforts to "Know it All"', *Washington Post*, 12 May 2014, <https://www.washingtonpost.com/opinions/no-place-to-hide-by-glenn-greenwald-on-the-nsas-sweeping-efforts-to-know-it-all/2014/05/12/dfa45dee-d628-11e3-8a78-8fe50322a72c_story.html> [accessed 2 July 2020].

35 'Surveillance Technologies', American Civil Liberties Union (ACLU), <https://www.aclu.org/issues/privacy-technology/surveillance-technologies> [accessed 2 July 2020].

36 René Girard, 'Triangular Desire', in *Deceit, Desire and the Novel: Self and Other in Literary Structure* (Baltimore, MD: Johns Hopkins University Press, 1965), pp. 1–52; René Girard, 'Hamlet's Dull Revenge', in *A Theater of Envy: William Shakespeare* (New York: Oxford University Press, 1991), pp. 271–89.

37 Russell Berman and Peter Thiel, 'German 270: Sovereignty and the Limits of Globalization and Technology', Stanford University, Winter Quarter 2019, <https://www.documentcloud.org/documents/5677718-Thiel-German-270-Syllabus.html> [accessed 2 October 2020].

38 Interview with Sam Wolfe (October 2019), a Stanford senior studying Comparative Literature and Political Science who took Peter Thiel's course 'Sovereignty and the Limits of Globalization and Technology' in 2018.

39 Sigmund Freud, *Civilization and Its Discontents* (Vienna: Internationaler Psychoanalytischer Verlag Wien, 1930).

40 Darren Lim and Victor Ferguson, 'Decoupling and the Technology Security Dilemma', *China Story Yearbook*, Australian National University, 2020.

41 Yoko Kubota and Liza Lin, 'Beijing Orders Agencies to Swap Out Foreign Tech for Chinese Gear', *Wall Street Journal*, 9 December 2019, <https://www.wsj.com/articles/beijing-orders-agencies-to-swap-out-foreign-tech-for-chinese-gear-11575921277> [accessed 2 July 2020]; Yuan Yang and Nian Liu, 'Beijing orders state offices to replace foreign PCs and software', *Financial Times*, 8 December 2019, <https://www.ft.com/content/b55fc6ee-1787-11ea-8d73-6303645ac406> [accessed 2 July 2020].

42 'The Clean Network', US Department of State, <https://www.state.gov/the-clean-network/> [accessed 2 July 2020]; 'US borrows from Beijing's playbook to decouple the Internet from China', Mercator Institute for China Studies, *MERICS China*

Briefing, 13 August 2020, <https://merics.org/en/newsletter/us-borrows-beijings-playbook-decouple-internet-china> [accessed 2 September 2020].

43 James Crabtree, 'Trump's TikTok battle heralds the ugly birth of a new splinternet', *Wired*, 21 September 2020, <https://www.wired.co.uk/article/tiktok-china-trump> [accessed 2 October 2020].

44 Yuan Yang and James Fontanella-Khan, 'Grindr sold by Chinese owner after US national security concerns', *Financial Times*, 7 March 2020, <https://www.ft.com/content/a32a740a-5fb3-11ea-8033-fa40a0d65a98> [accessed 3 October 2020].

45 James Crabtree, 'Trump's TikTok battle heralds the ugly birth of a new splinternet'.

CHAPTER TWO: CONNECTED MAN: HOW SOCIETY BECAME DIVIDED BY ENVY

1   Circe de Bruin, Lucia Hoenselaars and Machiel Spruijt, 'My Phone Helped Me With Everything', *Public History Amsterdam*, 2 December 2015, <http://publichistory.humanities.uva.nl/queercollection/my-phone-helped-me-with-everything/> [accessed 2 October 2020].

2   Rachel Halliburton, 'How Marine Le Pen is Winning France's Gay Vote', *The Spectator*, 15 August 2016.

3   Caroline Marie Lancaster, 'Not So Radical After All: Ideological Diversity Among Radical Right Supporters and Its Implications', *Political Studies*, September 2019.

4   Jaime Woo, *Meet Grindr: How one app changed the way we connect* (CreateSpace, 2013).

5   Emma Hope Allwood, 'What's Grindr's new agenda?', *Dazed*, 14 January 2016, <https://www.dazeddigital.com/fashion/article/29181/1/grindr-s-new-agenda> [accessed 4 October 2020].

6   Zygmunt Bauman and David Lyon, *Liquid Surveillance: A Conversation* (Cambridge: Polity, 2012).

7   Jean-Claude Kaufmann, *Love Online* (Cambridge: Polity, 2012).

8   'The New Grindr: Zero Feet Away', *CISION PR Newswire*, 1 October 2013, <https://www.prnewswire.com/news-releases/the-new-grindr-zero-feet-away-225991411.html> [accessed 8 October 2020].

9   Michael Rosenfeld, Reuben J. Thomas, Sonia Hausen, 'Disintermediating your friends: How online dating in the United States displaces other ways of meeting', *Proceedings of the National Academy of Sciences*, Volume 116, Issue 36, July 2019.

10 Alfie Bown, 'Tech is turning love into a right-wing game', *Guardian*, 3 May 2018, <https://www.theguardian.com/commentisfree/2018/may/03/tech-love-rightwing-game-facebook-dating-app> [accessed 4 October 2020]; 'Political dating sites are

hot', *Economist*, 26 January 2017, <https://www.economist.com/business/2017/01/ 26/political-dating-sites-are-hot> [accessed 5 October 2020]; Claire Downs, 'I tried the anti-feminist dating app for real "patriots"', *Daily Dot*, 19 September 2019, <https://www.dailydot.com/irl/patrio-dating-app/> [accessed 8 October 2020].

11   'Table FG4. Married Couple Family Groups, by Presence of Own Children in Specific Age Groups, and Age, Earnings, Education, and Race and Hispanic Origin of Both Spouses: 2010 (thousands)' in 'America's Families and Living Arrangements: 2010', United States Census Bureau, <https://www.census.gov/data/tables/2010/demo/fami lies/cps-2010.html> [accessed 8 October 2020].

12   Gregory A. Huber and Neil Malhotra, 'Political Homophily in Social Relationships: Evidence from Online Dating Behavior', *Journal of Politics*, January 2017.

13   Levi Boxell, Matthew Gentzkow and Jesse M. Shapiro, 'Greater Internet use is not associated with faster growth in political polarization among US demographic groups', *PNAS*, 114, no. 40 (2017), 10612–17.

14   Dhiraj Murthy, *Twitter: Social Communication in the Twitter Age* (Cambridge: Polity, 2013).

15   Freud, *Civilization and Its Discontents*.

16   J. D. Shadel, 'Grindr was the first big dating app for gay men: Now it's falling out of favor', *Washington Post*, 6 December 2018, <https://www.washingtonpost.com/life style/2018/12/06/grindr-was-first-big-dating-app-gay-men-now-its-falling-out-favor/> [accessed 8 October 2020].

17   Eleanor Hall, 'Misogyny isn't dying out, it just moved to WhatsApp', *GQ*, 21 November 2018, <https://www.gq-magazine.co.uk/article/whatsapp-groups> [accessed 8 October 2020].

18   Heather Webb, 'The Global Supply Chain of a Mobile Phone', *Ethical Consumer*, 15 October 2018, <https://www.ethicalconsumer.org/technology/global-supply-chain-mobile-phone> [accessed 8 June 2020]; Magdalena Petrova, 'We traced what it takes to make an iPhone, from its initial design to the components and raw materials needed to make it a reality', CNBC, 14 December 2018, <https://www.cnbc.com/ 2018/12/13/inside-apple-iphone-where-parts-and-materials-come-from.html> [accessed 8 June 2020].

19   Ulrich Beck, 'Living your own life in a runaway world: individualisation, globalisation and politics', in Will Hutton and Anthony Giddens (eds), *On the Edge* (New York: Vintage Books, 2001).

20   Bauman and Lyon, *Liquid Surveillance*.

21   See for instance Richard M. Perloff, 'Social Media Effects on Young Women's Body Image Concerns: Theoretical Perspectives and an Agenda for Research', *Sex Roles*, 71 (2014), 363–77, <https://doi.org/10.1007/s11199-014-0384-6>.

22 Leon Festinger, 'A theory of social comparison processes', *Human Relations*, 7, no. 2 (1954), 117–40, <doi:10.1177/001872675400700202>.

23 I am grateful to Professor Suzanne Skevington, a social psychologist at the University of Manchester, who shared her memories of working as a graduate student under the supervision of Henri Tajfel.

24 '5 Coolest Cars from Justin Bieber's Instagram', *Newswheel*, 18 January 2016, <https://thenewswheel.com/5-coolest-cars-from-justin-biebers-instagram/> [accessed 8 June 2020]; Greta Heggeness, 'Kelly Ripa & 7 Other Celebs Who Gave Us Rare Glimpses of Their Backyard Pools', *Purewow*, 5 October 2020, <https://www.purewow.com/entertainment/celebrity-backyard-pools> [accessed 8 November 2020]; Kim Kardashian's Instagram profile, <https://www.instagram.com/kimkardashian/> [accessed 8 November 2020].

25 Ivan Krastev, 'The Ambiguous Legacy of 1989', German Marshall Fund of the United States, 2 October 2015, <https://www.gmfus.org/blog/2015/10/02/ambiguous-legacy-1989> [accessed 8 October 2020].

26 Justyna Pawlak and Marcin Goe, 'For many voters in Poland, economic growth is not enough', Reuters, 20 October 2015.

27 Aleksandr Smolar, Interview with the author (2015).

28 Zygmunt Bauman, *Retropia* (Cambridge: Polity, 2017), p. 100.

29 John Naughton, 'From viral conspiracies to exam fiascos, algorithms come with serious side effects', *Guardian*, 6 September 2020, <https://www.theguardian.com/technology/2020/sep/06/from-viral-conspiracies-to-exam-fiascos-algorithms-come-with-serious-side-effects> [accessed 8 September 2020].

30 Shoshana Zuboff, *The Age of Surveillance Capitalism: The Fight for a Human Future at the New Frontier of Power* (New York: Public Affairs, 2019).

31 Neil Howe, 'A Special Price Just for You', *Forbes*, 17 November 2017, <https://www.forbes.com/sites/neilhowe/2017/11/17/a-special-price-just-for-you/#12f3b4bf90b3> [accessed 8 September 2020].

32 Rafi Mohammed, 'How Retailers Use Personalized Prices to Test What You're Willing to Pay', *Harvard Business Review*, 20 October 2017, <https://hbr.org/2017/10/how-retailers-use-personalized-prices-to-test-what-youre-willing-to-pay> [accessed 8 September 2020].

33 Marion Dakers, 'Uber knows that customers with dying batteries are more likely to accept surge pricing', *Telegraph*, 22 May 2016, <https://www.telegraph.co.uk/business/2016/05/22/uber-app-can-detect-when-a-users-phone-is-about-to-die/> [accessed 8 September 2020].

34 Kate Abnett, 'Will Personalised Pricing Take E-Commerce Back to the Bazaar?', *The Business of Fashion*, 20 March 2015, <https://www.businessoffashion.com/articles/

fashion-tech/personalised-pricing-turns-e-commerce-online-bazaar> [accessed 8 October 2020].

35 Joseph F. Coughlin, 'The "Internet of Things" Will Take Nudge Theory Too Far', *Big Think*, 27 March 2017, <https://bigthink.com/disruptive-demographics/the-internet-of-things-big-data-when-a-nudge-becomes-a-noodge> [accessed 8 October 2020].

36 Byung-Chul Han, *Psychopolitics: Neoliberalism and New Technologies of Power* (London/New York: Verso, 2017).

37 James Williams, *Stand Out of Our Light: Freedom and Resistance in the Attention Economy* (Cambridge: Cambridge University Press, 2018).

38 Kelsey Piper, 'AI could be a disaster for humanity. A top computer scientist thinks he has the solution', *Vox*, 26 October 2019, <https://www.vox.com/future-perfect/2019/10/26/20932289/ai-stuart-russell-human-compatible> [accessed 9 October 2020].

39 Jeffrey Dastin, 'Amazon scraps secret AI recruiting tool that showed bias against women', Reuters, 10 October 2018, <https://www.reuters.com/article/us-amazon-com-jobs-automation-insight-idUSKCN1MK08G> [accessed 8 October 2020].

40 Henry Kissinger, 'How the Enlightenment Ends', *Atlantic*, June 2018, <https://www.theatlantic.com/magazine/archive/2018/06/henry-kissinger-ai-could-mean-the-end-of-human-history/559124/> [accessed 11 October 2020].

41 Frank Pasquale, *The Black Box Society: The Secret Algorithms That Control Money and Information* (Cambridge MA: Harvard University Press, 2015).

42 Henry Kissinger, Eric Schmidt and Daniel Huttenlocher, 'The Metamorphosis', *Atlantic*, August 2019, <https://www.theatlantic.com/magazine/archive/2019/08/henry-kissinger-the-metamorphosis-ai/592771/> [accessed 11 October 2020].

43 Jamie Susskind, *Future Politics: Living Together in a World Transformed by Tech* (Oxford: Oxford University Press, 2018).

CHAPTER THREE: NATIONAL CULTURES OF UNPEACE: THE POLITICS OF TAKING BACK CONTROL

1 'Nearly two-thirds of Czechs oppose taking in war refugees: poll', Reuters, 15 February 2016, <http://www.reuters.com/article/us-europe-migrants-czech-poll-idUSKCN0VO1B3> [accessed 13 October 2020].

2 Dominik Jůn, 'Populist politician stages "Islamic State invasion" in Old Town Square', Radio Prague International, 22 August 2016, <http://www.radio.cz/en/section/cur raffrs/far-right-politician-stages-islamic-state-invasion-in-old-town-square> [accessed 25 July 2020].

3   Ibid.

4   Jan J. Hansen and Jürgen Osterhammel, *Decolonization: A Short History* (Princeton: Princeton University Press, 2017).

5   Manuel Castells, *The Internet Galaxy: Reflections on the Internet Business and Society* (Oxford University Press, 2003).

6   John B. Judis and Ruy Teixeira, *The Emerging Democratic Majority* (New York: Scribner, 2002).

7   'Transcript: Donald Trump's Victory Speech', *New York Times*, 9 November 2016, <http://www.nytimes.com/2016/11/10/us/politics/trump-speech-transcript.html?smprod=nytcore-iphone&smid=nytcore-iphone-share&_r=0> [accessed 25 July 2020].

8   Casey Newton, 'Read the full transcript of Mark Zuckerberg's leaked internal Facebook meetings', *Verge*, 1 October 2019, <https://www.theverge.com/2019/10/1/20892354/mark-zuckerberg-full-transcript-leaked-facebook-meetings?fbclid=IwAR2FfECh39oqMWQJdaq9cq38eOBABmZJaEbyyhcJprnOPjw18t2uRx6MGUM> [accessed 25 July 2020].

9   Ronald Inglehart and Pippa Norris, 'Trump, Brexit, and the Rise of Populism: Economic Have-Nots and Cultural Backlash', HKS Faculty Research Working Paper Series RWP16-026, August 2016, <https://www.hks.harvard.edu/publications/trump-brexit-and-rise-populism-economic-have-nots-and-cultural-backlash> [accessed 25 July 2020].

10 David Abernethy, *The Dynamics of Global Dominance: European Overseas Empires, 1415–1980* (New Haven, CT: Yale University Press, 2000).

11 Ibid.

12 Stuart Laycock, *All the Countries We've Ever Invaded: And the Few We Never Got Round To* (Cheltenham: The History Press, 2012).

13 Eric Hobsbawm, *Industry and Empire: From 1750 to the Present Day* (2nd edition) (London: Penguin Group, 1999).

14 Steve McCaskill, 'London Is "Most Connected" Major City In The World', *Silicon.co.uk*, 20 June 2016, <https://www.silicon.co.uk/networks/london-world-wi-fi-day-wba-193981> [accessed 25 July 2020].

15 'London is the world's most connected city, HK leads in Asia', *WIT*, 19 May 2016, <http://www.webintravel.com/rome2rio-global-connectivity-ranking/> [accessed 25 July 2020].

16 'The most globally connected financial centre: Always open and connected across the globe', <https://www.theglobalcity.uk/global-financial-centre> [accessed 25 July 2020].

17 Wolfgang Streek, *Buying Time: The Delayed Crisis of Democratic Capitalism* (London/New York: Verso Books, 2014).

18 See for example Morawiecki's 2017 interview for Polish TV (19 October 2017) where he quotes Berszidskij to be able to say that Poland can be seen as a 'foreign-owned' country, <https://www.youtube.com/watch?v=3b3y_1uJWIA> [accessed 25 July 2020].

19 Paul Streeten, 'The Use and Abuse of Models in Development Planning', in *The Frontiers of Development Studies* (London: Palgrave Macmillan, 1972), pp. 52–70.

20 Thomas Piketty, Emmanuel Saez and Gabriel Zucman, 'Distributional National Accounts: Methods and Estimates for the United States', *Quarterly Journal of Economics*, 11, no. 2 (2018), 553–609.

21 Susi Dennison, Mark Leonard and Adam Lury, 'What Europeans really feel: The battle for the political system', ECFR, 16 May 2019, <https://www.ecfr.eu/publications/summary/what_europeans_really_feel_the_battle_for_the_political_system_eu_election> [accessed 25 July 2020].

22 Will Davies, *Nervous States: How Feeling Took Over the World* (London: Jonathan Cape, 2018).

23 Dennison, Leonard and Lury, 'What Europeans really feel'.

CHAPTER FOUR: THE GEOPOLITICS OF CONNECTIVITY: WHY COUNTRIES COMPETE RATHER THAN WORK TOGETHER

1 Norman Angell, the only person to have been awarded the Nobel Peace Prize for publishing a book, argued in 1910 that the expansion of free trade would create greater interdependence between states and along with improved education would make war irrational (because of the danger of mutual destruction) and uncivilized. The outbreak in August 1914 of the First World War appeared to refute his main thesis. Similar arguments have been made about Richard Nixon's opening to China, Willy Brandt's *Ostpolitik*, and Henry Kissinger's strategy of détente with the Soviet Union.

2 Thomas Friedman, *The World Is Flat: A Brief History of the Twenty-first Century* (3rd edition) (London: Picador, 2007).

3 Albert Hirschman, *National Power and the Structure of Foreign Trade* (Berkeley and Los Angeles: University of California Press, 1945).

4 Dale Copeland claims that when leaders have positive expectations of the future

trade environment, they want to remain at peace in order to secure the economic benefits that enhance long-term power. When, however, these expectations turn negative, leaders are likely to fear a loss of access to raw materials and markets, giving them more incentive to initiate crises to protect their commercial interests. Dale C. Copeland, 'Economic Interdependence and War: A Theory of Trade Expectations', *International Security*, 20, no. 4 (1996), 5–41.

5   Ibid.

6   Erik Gartzke, 'Interdependence really is complex', University of California San Diego, February 2010, <http://pages.ucsd.edu/~egartzke/papers/complexinterdep_02242010.pdf> [accessed 13 October 2020].

7   Center for Strategic and International Studies, 'The Grayzone Project', <https://www.csis.org/grayzone> [accessed 25 July 2020]; Raphael S. Cohen and others, *The Future of Warfare in 2030: Project Overview and Conclusions*, RAND, 2020, <https://www.rand.org/pubs/research_reports/RR2849z1.html> [accessed 25 November 2020].

8   Helmi Noman, 'Internet Censorship and the Intraregional Geopolitical Conflicts in the Middle East and North Africa', *Berkman Klein Center Research Publication No. 1* (2019).

9   Michael Sexton and Eliza Campbell, *Cyber War & Cyber Peace in the Middle East: Digital Conflict in the Cradle of Civilization* (Middle East Institute, October 2020).

10 Ibid.

11 Christopher Bing and Raphael Satter, 'Exclusive: Trump campaign targeted by Iran-linked hackers – sources', Reuters, 4 October 2019, <https://www.reuters.com/article/us-cyber-security-iran-trump-exclusive/exclusive-trump-campaign-targeted-by-iran-linked-hackers-sources-idUSKBN1WJ2B4> [accessed 25 November 2020].

12 Adam Goldman, 'Spy Betrayed U.S. to Work for Iran, Charges Say', *New York Times*, 13 February 2019, <https://www.nytimes.com/2019/02/13/world/middleeast/air-force-monica-elfriede-witt-iran.html> [accessed 28 November 2020]; 'Ex-US Air Force officer Monica Witt charged with spying for Iran', BBC News, 13 February 2019, <https://www.bbc.com/news/world-us-canada-47231777> [accessed 28 November 2020]; 'Monica Elfriede Witt', *FBI Most Wanted*, 13 February 2019, <https://www.fbi.gov/wanted/counterintelligence/monica-elfriede-witt> [accessed 28 November 2020].

13 'Cyber Operations Tracker', Council on Foreign Relations, <https://www.cfr.org/cyber-operations/> [accessed 28 January 2021].

14 Ariane M. Tabatabai, 'Syria Changed the Iranian Way of War', *Foreign Affairs*, 16 August 2019.

15 'Twitter Suspends 90,000 Accounts Used to Spread Saudi Spam', *Bloomberg*, 20 December 2019.

CHAPTER FIVE: AN ANATOMY OF UNPEACE: HOW GLOBALIZATION WAS TURNED INTO A WEAPON

1 'Turkey's charismatic pro-Islamic leader', BBC Europe, 4 November 2002, <http://news.bbc.co.uk/2/hi/europe/2270642.stm> [accessed 13 October 2020].

2 'Erdoğan's new sultanate', Economist, 4 February 2016, <http://www.economist.com/news/special-report/21689871-under-recep-tayip-erdogan-and-his-ak-party-turkey-has-become-richer-and-more-confident> [accessed 25 October 2020].

3 Kathrin Hille and Laura Pitel, 'Russia and Turkey seek to repair ties after Putin and Erdoğan phone call', Financial Times, 29 June 2016, <https://www.ft.com/content/210057f2-3df6-11e6-8716-a4a71e8140b0> [accessed 21 October 2020].

4 Dan Drezner, The Sanctions Paradox: Economic Statecraft and International Relations (Cambridge: Cambridge University Press, 1999).

5 Joanna Diane Caytas, 'Weaponizing Finance: U.S. and European Options, Tools, and Policies', Columbia Journal of European Law, 23, no. 441 (2017).

6 Ellie Geranmayeh, 'Secondary reach of US sanctions in Europe: how far is too far?', ECFR Blog, 12 June 2014, <http://www.ecfr.eu/blog/entry/secondary_reach_of_us_sanctions_in_europe_how_far_is_too_far> [accessed 17 February 2020].

7 Joanna Diane Caytas, 'Weaponizing Finance'; Eric Lichtblau and James Risen, 'Bank Data Is Sifted by U.S. in Secret to Block Terror', New York Times, 23 June 2006, <https://www.nytimes.com/2006/06/23/washington/23intel.html> [accessed 16 October 2020].

8 'Facing the sanctions challenge in financial services: A global sanctions compliance study', Deloitte, 2009, <https://www2.deloitte.com/content/dam/Deloitte/ru/Documents/financial-services/Facing%20the%20sanctions%20challenge%20in%20financial%20services.pdf> [accessed 18 February 2020].

9 Juan Zarate, Treasury's War: The Unleashing of a New Era of Financial Warfare (New York: Public Affairs, 2013), p. 244.

10 Greg Satell, 'Here's How Obama's Russia Sanctions Will Destroy Vladimir Putin', Forbes, 28 April 2014, <http://www.forbes.com/sites/gregsatell/2014/04/28/ heres-how-obamas-sanctions-will-destroy-vladimir-putin/> [accessed 18 February 2020].

11 Ibid.

12 'The struggle over chips enters a new phase', Economist, 23 January 2021.

13 Nisha Gopalan, 'China May Dismiss U.S. Sanctions. Its Banks Can't', Bloomberg, 14 August 2020, <https://www.bloomberg.com/opinion/articles/2020-08-13/china-banks-bowing-to-u-s-sanctions-shows-dollar-s-power> [accessed 18 December 2020].

14 Mark Leonard (ed.), *Connectivity Wars*.

15 Li Keqiang, 'China deepens strategy of domestic demand expansion in the course of reform and opening-up', China.org.cn, 4 March 2012, <http://www.china.org.cn/china/2012-03/04/content_24801231.htm> [accessed 18 February 2020].

16 Dimitri Simes, 'China and Russia ditch dollar in move towards "financial alliance"', *Financial Times*, 17 August 2020, <https://www.ft.com/content/8421b6a2-1dc6-4747-b2e9-1bbfb7277747> [accessed 19 November 2020].

17 Steven Blockmans, 'Extraterritorial sanctions with a Chinese trademark', CEPS, 26 January 2021,<https://www.ceps.eu/ceps-publications/extraterritorial-sanctions-with-a-chinese-trademark/> [accessed 19 November 2020].

18 Hirschman, *National Power and The Structure of Foreign Trade*.

19 Robert D. Atkinson, 'A Remarkable Resemblance', *The International Economy*, Fall 2020.

20 Kate Buck, 'I've seen starving North Korean women executed for eating their own children', *Metro*, 27 February 2019, <https://metro.co.uk/2019/02/27/ive-seen-starving-north-korean-women-executed-for-eating-their-own-children-8726479/> [accessed 21 November 2020].

21 Matthias Neuenkirch and Florian Neumeier, 'The Impact of UN and US Economic Sanctions on GDP Growth', Forschungsschwerpunkt Internationale Wirtschaft (FIW) Working Paper 138 (January 2015), <https://www.fiw.ac.at/fileadmin/Documents/Publikationen/Working_Paper/N_138_NeuenkirchNeumeier.pdf> [accessed 16 February 2020].

22 Rune Friberg Lyme, 'Sanctioning Assad's Syria: Mapping the economic, socioeconomic and political repercussions of the international sanctions imposed on Syria since March 2011', Danish Institute for International Studies (DIIS) Report 13 (2012), <https://www.diis.dk/files/media/publications/import/extra/rp2012-13_sanctioning_assads_syria_web_1.pdf> [accessed 16 February 2020], p. 60; Rania Khalek, 'US and EU Sanctions are Punishing Ordinary Syrians and Crippling Aid Work, U.N. report reveals', *The Intercept*, 28 September 2016, <https://theintercept.com/2016/09/28/u-s-sanctions-are-punishing-ordinary-syrians-and-crippling-aid-work-u-n-report-reveals/> [accessed 16 February 2020].

23 'World Economic Outlook: Global Manufacturing Downturn, Rising Trade Barriers', IMF, October 2019, <https://www.imf.org/en/Publications/WEO/Issues/2019/10/01/world-economic-outlook-october-2019> [accessed 16 February 2020], p. 14.

24 'Inflation rate, average consumer prices', IMF, 2020, <https://www.imf.org/external/datamapper/PCPIPCH@WEO/WEOWORLD/VEN> [accessed 16 November 2020]; Emilio Fernandez Corugedo and Jaime Guajardo, 'For Venezuela's Neighbors, Mass Migration Brings Economic Costs and Benefits', IMF Blog, 21 November 2019, <https://blogs.imf.org/2019/11/21/for-venezuelas-neighbors-mass-migration-brings-economic-costs-and-benefits/> [accessed 16 February 2020].

25 'Venezuelan Refugee and Migrant Crisis: Overview', IOM, <https://www.iom.int/venezuela-refugee-and-migrant-crisis> [accessed 16 December 2020].

26 Jerg Gutmann, Matthias Neuenkirch and Florian Neumeier, 'Sanctioned to Death? The Impact of Economic Sanctions on Life Expectancy and its Gender Gap', University of Trier, Research Papers in Economics, no. 6/17 (September 2018), <https://www.uni-trier.de/fileadmin/fb4/prof/VWL/EWF/Research_Papers/2017-06.pdf> [accessed 16 February 2020].

27 Abbas Alnasrawi, 'Iraq: economic sanctions and consequences, 1990–2000', Third World Quarterly, 22, no. 2 (2001), 205–18.

28 Ibid.

29 Kee B. Park, Miles Kim and Jessup Jong, 'The Human Costs of UN Sanctions and Funding Shortfalls for Humanitarian Aid in North Korea', 38 North, 22 August 2019, <https://www.38north.org/2019/08/parkkimjong082219/> [accessed 17 February 2020].

30 Mark Weisbrot and Jeffrey Sachs, 'Economic Sanctions as Collective Punishment: The Case of Venezuela', Center for Economic and Policy Research, April 2019, <https://cepr.net/images/stories/reports/venezuela-sanctions-2019-04.pdf> [accessed 17 February 2020].

31 Ibid., p. 11.

32 Marton Dunai, 'Hungary welcomes wealthy Chinese despite migrant hostility', Reuters, 5 October 2016, <http://www.reuters.com/article/us-europe-migrants-china-hungary-idUSKCN1250RN> [accessed 20 February 2020].

33 Robert Velkey, 'News About Injured Survivors of the Verona Bus Accident', Hungary Today, 28 February 2017, <http://hungarytoday.hu/news/91762> [accessed 18 February 2020].

34 Ibid.

35 Csaba Tóth, 'Full text of Viktor Orbán's speech at Băile Tuşnad (Tusnádfürdő) of 26 July 2014', The Budapest Beacon, 29 July 2014, <https://budapestbeacon.com/full-text-of-viktor-orbans-speech-at-baile-tusnad-tusnadfurdo-of-26-july-2014/> [accessed 10 February 2020].

36 Jonathan E. Hillman, 'How Big Is China's Belt and Road?', Center for Strategic and International Studies, 3 April 2019, <https://www.csis.org/analysis/how-big-chinas-belt-and-road> [accessed 10 April 2020].

37 Dragan Pavlićević and Agatha Kratz, 'Testing the China Threat paradigm: China's high-speed railway diplomacy in Southeast Asia', The Pacific Review, 31, no. 2 (2018), 151–68.

38 Keith Barney, 'High speed rail could bankrupt Laos, but it'll keep China happy',

The Conversation, 7 April 2014, <http://theconversation.com/high-speed-rail-could-bankrupt-laos-but-itll-keep-china-happy-22657> [accessed 10 February 2020].

39 Although the researcher Agatha Kratz reports that many security people she interviewed in the region were sanguine about the use of railways in today's wars because they can be broken down with a few well-targeted missiles (email exchange with the author, September 2020).

40 James Kynge and Jonathan Wheatley, 'China pulls back from the world: rethinking Xi's "project of the century"', *Financial Times*, 11 December 2020, <https://www.ft.com/content/d9bd8059-d05c-4e6f-968b-1672241ec1f6> [accessed 21 February 2021].

41 Jude Blanchette and Jonathan E. Hillman, 'China's Digital Silk Road after the Coronavirus', Center for Strategic and International Studies, 13 April 2020, <https://www.csis.org/analysis/chinas-digital-silk-road-after-coronavirus> [accessed 21 February 2021].

42 David Sanger, *The Perfect Weapon: War, Sabotage, and Fear in the Cyber Age* (Melbourne: Scribe Publications, 2018).

43 'Zhu Hua', *FBI Most Wanted*, 20 December 2018, <https://www.fbi.gov/wanted/cyber/zhu-hua> [accessed 10 February 2020].

44 'APT10 was managed by the Tianjin bureau of the Chinese Ministry of State Security', *Intrusion Truth*, 15 August 2018, <https://intrusiontruth.wordpress.com/2018/08/15/apt10-was-managed-by-the-tianjin-bureau-of-the-chinese-ministry-of-state-security/> [accessed 10 February 2020].

45 Brian Barrett, 'How China's Elite Hackers Stole the World's Most Valuable Secrets', *Wired*, 20 December 2018, <https://www.wired.com/story/doj-indictment-chinese-hackers-apt10/> [accessed 10 February 2020].

46 Henry Farrell and Abraham L. Newman, 'Weaponized Interdependence: How global economic networks shape state coercion', *International Security*, 44, no. 1 (2019), 42–79.

47 Farrell and Newman quoted in Michael Hirsch, 'How America's Top Companies Created the Surveillance State', *National Journal*, 26 July 2013, <http://www.nextgov.com/cio-briefing/2013/07/analysis-how-americas-top-tech-companies-created-surveillance-state/67490/> [accessed 16 October 2020].

48 Alex Hern, 'WannaCry, Petya, NotPetya: how ransomware hit the big time in 2017', *Guardian*, 30 December 2017, <https://www.theguardian.com/technology/2017/dec/30/wannacry-petya-notpetya-ransomware> [accessed 10 February 2020].

49 'Chinese Cyber Spies Hack Taiwan Ruling Party: FireEye', *Security Week*, 2 June 2016,<https://www.securityweek.com/chinese-cyber-spies-hack-taiwan-ruling-party-fireeye> [accessed 13 February 2020].

50 Herbert Lin, 'The Existential Threat From Cyber Enabled Information Warfare', *Bulletin of the Atomic Scientists*, 75 (June 2019), 187–96.

51 Ibid.

52 Christopher Wray, 'The FBI and the National Security Threat Landscape: The Next Paradigm Shift', *FBI Speeches*, 26 April 2019, <https://www.fbi.gov/news/speeches/the-fbi-and-the-national-security-threat-landscape-the-next-paradigm-shift> [accessed 13 February 2020].

53 Kristin Shi-Kupfer and Mareike Ohlberg, 'China's Digital Rise: Challenges for Europe', *MERICS Papers on China*, 7, April 2019.

54 James Kynge and Nian Liu, 'From AI to facial recognition: how China is setting the rules in new tech', *Financial Times*, 7 October 2020, <https://www.ft.com/content/188d86df-6e82-47eb-a134-2e1e45c777b6> [accessed 16 December 2020].

55 Ibid.

56 Adrian Shahbaz, 'Freedom on the Net 2018: The Rise of Digital Authoritarianism', Freedom House, 2018, <https://freedomhouse.org/report/freedom-net/2018/rise-digital-authoritarianism> [accessed 16 December 2020].

57 Kieron O'Hara and Wendy Hall, 'Four Internets: the Geopolitics of Digital Governance', *CIGI Papers Series*, 7 December 2018, <https://www.cigionline.org/publications/four-internets-geopolitics-digital-governance> [accessed 14 July 2020].

58 'Erdoğan: Daha ileri giderseniz sınır kapıları açılır', *Hürriyet*, 25 November 2016, <http://www.hurriyet.com.tr/erdogan-daha-ileri-giderseniz-sinir-kapilarini-acariz-40288025> [accessed 14 July 2020].

59 'Turkish president threatens to send millions of Syrian refugees to EU', *Guardian*, 12 February 2016, <https://www.theguardian.com/world/2016/feb/12/turkish-president-threatens-to-send-millions-of-syrian-refugees-to-eu> [accessed 14 July 2020].

60 Kelly M. Greenhill, *Weapons of Mass Migration: Forced Displacement, Coercion, and Foreign Policy* (Ithaca, NY: Cornell University Press, 2011).

61 Sholto Byrnes, 'Colonel Gaddafi warns Europe over "turning black"', *New Statesman*, 1 December 2010, <https://www.newstatesman.com/blogs/the-staggers/2010/12/obama-gaddafi-black-europe> [accessed 14 July 2020].

62 Greenhill, *Weapons of Mass Migration*.

63 Kelly M. Greenhill, 'Migration as a Weapon in Theory and in Practice', *Military Review*, November/December 2016, p. 27.

64 Frank Mattern and others, 'Europe's New Refugees: A Road Map for Better Integration Outcomes', McKinsey Global Institute, 1 December 2016, p. 1.

65 Michael A. Clemens, 'Economics and Emigration: Trillion-Dollar Bills on the Side-walk?', *Journal of Economic Perspectives*, 25, no. 3 (2011).

66 'Migrant crisis: Russia and Syria "weaponising" migration', *BBC News*, 2 March 2016, <http://www.bbc.com/news/world-europe-35706238> [accessed 14 July 2020].

67 'Overview of Rules on Entry and Residence of Nationals of CIS Member Countries in the Russian Federation', V. I. Vernadsky Crimean Federal University, <https://eng.cfuv. ru/viza-i-migracionnaya-podderzhka/overview-of-rules-on-entry-and-residence-of-nationals-of-cis-member-countries-in-the-russian-federation> [accessed 14 July 2020]; 'Tajik Migrants with Re-entry Bans to the Russian Federation', IOM, 2014, <https://pub lications.iom.int/books/tajik-migrants-re-entry-bans-russian-federation> [accessed 14 July 2020].

68 Mark Leonard, 'Getting a Grip on Migration', *Project Syndicate*, 17 June 2016, <https:// www.project-syndicate.org/onpoint/getting-a-grip-on-migration-by-mark-leonard-2016-06> [accessed 14 October 2020].

69 Jonathan Woetzel and others, 'People on the move: global migration's impact and opportunity', McKinsey Global Institute, December 2016, p. 1.

70 Ibid., p. 13.

71 Ibid.

72 Dan Senor and Saul Singer, *Start-up Nation: The Story of Israel's Economic Miracle* (New York: Twelve, 2009).

73 'Number of foreign fighters in Iraq and Syria doubles in a year, report finds', *Guardian*, 8 December 2015, <https://www.theguardian.com/world/2015/dec/08/isis-foreign-fighters-iraq-syria-doubles-report> [accessed 17 October 2020].

74 Richard Hall, 'Isis caliphate defeated: Victory declared as Islamic State loses last of its territory', *Independent*, 23 March 2019, <https://www.independent.co.uk/news/ world/middle-east/isis-caliphate-over-islamic-state-territory-lose-syria-iraq-terrorists-jihadis-a8781896.html> [accessed 14 October 2020].

75 Jessica Stern and J. M. Berger, 'Thugs wanted – bring your own boots: how Isis attracts foreign fighters to its twisted utopia', *Guardian*, 9 March 2015, <https://www. theguardian.com/world/2015/mar/09/how-isis-attracts-foreign-fighters-the-state-of-terror-book> [accessed 14 October 2020].

76 John Sutter and Lawrence Davidson, 'Teen tells climate negotiators they aren't mature enough', CNN, 17 December 2018, <https://edition.cnn.com/2018/12/16/world/greta-thunberg-cop24/index.html> [accessed 14 October 2020].

77 Linda Givetash, 'Australian wildfires declared among the "worst wildlife disasters in modern history"', *NBC News*, 28 July 2020, <https://www.nbcnews.com/news/

world/australian-wildfires-declared-among-worst-wildlife-disasters-modern-history-n1235071> [accessed 14 October 2020].

78 Naomi Klein, '"We have a once-in-century chance": Naomi Klein on how we can fight the climate crisis', *Guardian*, 14 September 2019, <https://www.theguardian.com/books/2019/sep/14/crisis-talk-green-new-deal-naomi-klein> [accessed 14 December 2020].

79 'About us', Rainforest Concern, <https://www.rainforestconcern.org/about-us> [accessed 14 December 2020].

80 E. S. Brondizio, J. Settele, S. Díaz, and H. T. Ngo (eds), *Global assessment report on biodiversity and ecosystem services of the Intergovernmental Science-Policy Platform on Biodiversity and Ecosystem Services* (Bonn: IPBES secretariat, 2019).

81 Nina Tannenwald, 'Life Beyond Arms Control: Moving Toward a Global Regime of Nuclear Restraint and Responsibility', American Academy of Arts and Sciences, 2020.

82 Laurens Cerulus and Eline Schaart, 'How the UN migration pact got trolled', *Politico*, 3 January 2019, <https://www.politico.eu/article/united-nations-migration-pact-how-got-trolled/> [accessed 4 April 2021].

CHAPTER SIX: THE NEW TOPOGRAPHY OF POWER

1 Yuval Noah Harari, *Homo Sapiens: A Brief History of Humankind* (London: Harvill Secker, 2014).

2 Jürgen Osterhammel, *The Transformation of the World: A Global History of the Nineteenth Century* (Princeton: Princeton University Press, 2014).

3 Eric Hobsbawm, *The Age of Revolution: Europe 1789–1848* (London: Weidenfeld & Nicolson, 1962).

4 Vanessa Ogle, *The Global Transformation of Time 1870–1950* (Cambridge, MA: Harvard University Press, 2015).

5 Ibid.

6 Ibid.

7 Osterhammel, *The Transformation of the World*.

8 Friedman, *The World Is Flat*.

9 For a complete introduction to the basic concepts of network science see M. E. J. Newman, *Networks: An Introduction* (New York: Oxford University Press, 2010).

10 Anne-Marie Slaughter, 'The Real New World Order', *Foreign Affairs*, September/

October 1997, <https://www.foreignaffairs.com/articles/1997-09-01/real-new-world-order> [accessed 27 July 2020].

11   A lot of amazing work has been done on networks. I want to particularly mention here: Anne-Marie Slaughter, *The Chessboard and the Web: Strategies of Connection in a Networked World* (New Haven, CT: Yale University Press, 2017); Parag Khanna, *Connectography: Mapping the Global Network Revolution* (London: Weidenfeld & Nicolson, 2017); Niall Ferguson, *The Square and the Tower: Networks, Hierarchies and the Struggle for Global Power* (London: Penguin, 2018); Albert-László Barabási, *Linked: How Everything Is Connected to Everything Else and What It Means for Business, Science and Everyday Life* (New York: Penguin, 2002); Manuel Castells's three-volume Information Age trilogy: *The Rise of Network Society* (Oxford: Blackwell, 1996), *The Power of Identity* (1997) and *End of Millennium* (1998); Manuel Castells, *Communication Power* (Oxford University Press, 2009); Manuel Castells, *The Internet Galaxy: Reflections on the Internet Business and Society* (Oxford University Press, 2003); Manuel Castells, *Networks of Outrage and Hope: Social Movements in the Internet Age* (Cambridge: Polity, 2015).

12   John F. Padgett and Walter W. Powell, 'The Problem of Emergence', in *The Emergence of Organizations and Markets* (Princeton, NJ: Princeton University Press, 2012), p. 2.

13   Sulzhan Bali, Kearsley A. Stewart and Muhammad Ali Pate, 'Long shadow of fear in an epidemic: fearonomic effects of Ebola on the private sector in Nigeria', *BMJ Global Health*, 2016, <http://gh.bmj.com/content/1/3/e000111> [accessed 27 October 2020].

14   Ibid.

15   Miller McPherson, Lynn Smith-Lovin and James M. Cook, 'Birds of a Feather: Homophily in Social Networks', *Annual Review of Sociology*, 27, no. 1 (2001), 415–44.

16   Barabási, *Linked*.

17   Tom Goodwin, 'The Battle Is For The Customer Interface', *Tech Crunch*, 3 March 2015,<https://techcrunch.com/2015/03/03/in-the-age-of-disintermediation-the-battle-is-all-for-the-customer-interface/> [accessed 27 October 2020].

18   Anne-Marie Slaughter, 'How to Succeed in the Networked World: A Grand Strategy for the Digital Age', *Foreign Affairs*, November/December 2016, <https://www.foreignaffairs.com/articles/world/2016-10-04/how-succeed-networked-world> [accessed 13 October 2020].

19   Slaughter, *The Chessboard and the Web*.

20   Barabási, *Linked*.

21   Peter Csermely and others, 'Structure and dynamics of core/periphery networks', *Journal of Complex Networks*, 1 (2013), 93–123, <https://arxiv.org/pdf/1309.6928.pdf> [accessed 27 October 2020].

22 Joshua Cooper Ramo, *The Seventh Sense: Power, Fortune, and Survival in the Age of Networks* (Boston, MA: Little, Brown & Company, 2016).

23 Howard French, *China's Second Continent: How a Million Migrants Are Building a New Empire in Africa* (London: Vintage, 2015).

CHAPTER SEVEN: EMPIRES OF CONNECTIVITY

1 Douglas McGray, 'The Marshall Plan', *Wired*, 2 January 2003, <https://www.wired.com/2003/02/marshall/> [accessed 14 October 2020].

2 'The dragon's new teeth', *Economist*, 7 April 2012, <http://www.economist.com/node/21552193?fsrc=nlw per cent7Chig per cent7C4-5-2012 per cent7C1303226 per cent7C3 6310463> [accessed 14 October 2020].

3 Laura Rosenberger, 'Making Cyberspace Safe for Democracy: The New Landscape of Information Competition', *Foreign Affairs*, May/June 2020, <https://www.foreign affairs.com/articles/china/2020-04-13/making-cyberspace-safe-democracy> [accessed 27 November 2020].

4 Shawn Donnan, 'Biden Wants a Foreign Policy That Puts Middle-Class America First', *Bloomberg*, 4 February 2021, <https://www.bloomberg.com/news/articles/2021-02-04/bidens-foreign-policy-focuses-on-middle-class-americans> [accessed 15 February 2021]; Salman Ahmed and others, 'Making U.S. Foreign Policy Work Better for the Middle Class', Carnegie Endowment for International Peace, 23 September 2020, <https://carnegieendowment.org/2020/09/23/making-u.s.-foreign-policy-work-better-for-middle-class-pub-82728> [accessed 27 November 2020].

5 'Exclusive Interview: Jake Sullivan, Biden's National Security Adviser', *NPR Politics Podcast*, 30 December 2020, <https://www.npr.org/transcripts/951503916> [accessed 3 January 2021].

6 'The Biden Plan to rebuild U.S. supply chains and ensure the U.S. does not face future shortages of critical equipment', joebiden.com <https://joebiden.com/supply chains/> [accessed 27 November 2020].

7 Kurt M. Campbell and Jake Sullivan, 'Competition Without Catastrophe: How America Can Both Challenge and Coexist With China', *Foreign Affairs*, September/October 2019, <https://www.foreignaffairs.com/articles/china/competition-with-china-without-catastrophe> [accessed 27 November 2020].

8 Leonard, *What Does China Think?*

9 Qin Yaqing, *A Relational Theory of World Politics* (Cambridge: Cambridge University Press, 2018).

10 Emilian Kavalski, 'Guanxi or What is the Chinese for Relational Theory of World Politics', *International Relations of the Asia-Pacific*, 18, no. 3 (2018), 397–420.

11 Qin, *A Relational Theory of World Politics*.

12 Kevin Yao, 'What we know about China's "dual circulation" economic strategy', Reuters, 15 September 2020, <https://www.reuters.com/article/china-economy-transformation-explainer-idUSKBN2600B5> [accessed 16 October 2020].

13 Julian Gewirtz, 'The Chinese Reassessment of Interdependence', *China Leadership Monitor*, 1 June 2020, <https://www.prcleader.org/gewirtz> [accessed 16 October 2020].

14 Ibid.

15 'EU Antitrust Boss Flags Facebook Crypto Libra for Monopoly Risks – CCN Markets', *Litecoin Investor*, 5 September 2019, <https://litecoininvestor.net/eu-facebook-crypto-libra-monopoly-risk/> [accessed 16 October 2020].

16 Pascal Lamy, 'The New World of Trade', ECIPE, May 2015, <https://ecipe.org/publications/new-world-trade/> [accessed 20 October 2020].

17 Anu Bradford, *The Brussels Effect: How the European Union Rules the World* (Oxford: Oxford University Press, 2020).

18 Zaki Laïdi, *Norms Over Force: The Enigma of European Power* (London: Palgrave Macmillan, 2008).

19 Nikita Kwatra and Sriharsha Devulapalli, 'By distancing China in tech, India may be shooting itself in the foot', *Mint*, 26 September 2020, <https://www.livemint.com/news/india/by-distancing-china-in-tech-india-may-be-shooting-itself-in-the-foot-11601045308847.html> [accessed 20 October 2020].

20 'The new scramble for Africa: This time, the winners could be Africans themselves', *Economist*, 9 March 2019, <https://www.economist.com/leaders/2019/03/07/the-new-scramble-for-africa> [accessed 24 October 2020].

CONCLUSION: DISARMING CONNECTIVITY: A MANIFESTO

1 Yansheng Ma Lum and Raymond Mun Kong Lum, *Sun Yat-sen in Hawaii: Activities and Supporters* (Honolulu: University of Hawaii Press, 1999).

2 'Recovery from Codependency', *Good Therapy*, 21 November 2019, <https://www.goodtherapy.org/learn-about-therapy/issues/codependency/recovery> [accessed 2 November 2020].

3 John Boswell and others, 'Place-based Politics and Nested Deprivation in the U.K.: Beyond Cities-towns, "Two Englands" and the "Left Behind"', *Journal of Representative Democracy*, 24 April 2020, <https://doi.org/10.1080/00344893.2020.1751258>.

4 'US–China Trade Relations: A way forward', US–China Trade Policy Working

Group, 27 October 2019, <https://en.nsd.pku.edu.cn/docs/20191102095843918441. pdf> [accessed 2 November 2020].

5   Paul Scheffer, 'Het multiculturele drama', *NRC Handelsblad*, 19 January 2000, <https://retro.nrc.nl/W2/Lab/Multicultureel/scheffer.html> [accessed 2 November 2020].

6   Paul Scheffer, *Immigrant Nations* (Cambridge: Polity, 2011).

7   Jonathan Haidt, 'When and Why Nationalism Beats Globalism', *The American Interest,* July 2016.

8   See for example Mark Zuckerberg, 'Building Global Community', Facebook, 16 February 2017, <https://www.facebook.com/notes/mark-zuckerberg/building-global-community/10154544292806634/> [accessed 2 November 2020]; Cal Newport, *Digital Minimalism: Choosing a Focused Life in a Noisy World* (London: Portfolio, 2019); Jenna Clark, 'What Makes Technology Good or Bad for Us?', *Greater Good Magazine*, 2 May 2019, <https://greatergood.berkeley.edu/article/item/what_makes_technology_good_or_bad_for_us> [accessed 2 December 2020].

9   Anthony Giddens, 'A magna carta for the digital age', *Washington Post*, 2 May 2018, <https://www.washingtonpost.com/news/theworldpost/wp/2018/05/02/artificial-intelligence/> [accessed 2 December 2020].

INDEX

ABOUT THE AUTHOR

Mark Leonard is the Director and Co-founder of the European Council on Foreign Relations, a council of 300 European leaders including serving and former presidents, prime ministers, economics and foreign ministers, and the author of *Why Europe Will Run the 21st Century* (2005) and *What Does China Think?* (2008). He lives in London and Berlin.